Advance praise for *Becoming Like a Cl...*

"Those of us who have dedicated our lives ω ...
dren often use Jesus' words about the necessity of becoming ...
to enter God's kingdom as a justification for all we do. Jesus respected
children—so we should too. However, no one up until now has explored
these words of Jesus so thoroughly and with such breadth as Jerome Berryman does in this book. This brilliant explication of scripture using psychology, theology, history, and story opens up new ways of thinking about
processes of faith formation. This book will challenge your mind and
expand your thinking and practice around faith formation for all ages."

—The Reverend Dr. Ivy Beckwith, Faith Formation
Team Leader, United Church of Christ, and co-author
of *Children's Ministry in the Way of Jesus*

"Berryman is simply brilliant. He seems to have read everyone who
has studied children, introduces us to this vast, rich literature across
disciplines, and in this *tour de force* gives us a theology, spirituality,
and ethic that is grounded in the godly play of becoming children of
wonder, gratitude, and creativity."

—Timothy F. Sedgwick, PhD, Professor of Christian Ethics
at Virginia Theological Seminary

"Jerome Berryman challenges the church to open its eyes and see like a
child, and challenges theologians to discover a whole new and challenging spirit in which to understand their craft. But most importantly, he
turns our view of God upside down and makes us wonder how things
would be if God were not the aloof, distant, bearded patriarch but were
in truth a wide-eyed, ingenuous, trusting child. Just imagine—and be lost
in wonder."

—The Reverend Dr. Samuel Wells, Vicar,
St. Martin in the Fields, London

"I can think of no one who has done more to increase awareness of the
spiritual aptitude of children than Jerome Berryman. In this latest deeply
thoughtful work, he argues Jesus' position that to become mature we
must be 'fully adult and fully children at the same time.' He challenges
us to see children as 'parables of action.' If nothing else, this book will
change your view of children and the Kingdom of God. And that's a
good thing."

—Scottie May, PhD, Associate Professor Emerita, Department
of Christian Formation and Ministry, Wheaton College

Becoming Like a Child

The Curiosity of Maturity beyond the Norm

JEROME W. BERRYMAN

Church Publishing
NEW YORK

Church Publishing, 19 East 34th Street, New York, NY 10016
www.churchpublishing.org

Cover design by Jennifer Kopec, 2Pug Design
Typeset by Rose Design

Library of Congress Cataloging-in-Publication Data

A record of this book is available from the Library of Congress.

ISBN-13: 978-0-8192-3323-3 (pbk.)
ISBN-13: 978-0-8192-3324-0 (ebook)

Printed in the United States of America

For and because of Thea
and the children of the world—as always . . .

CONTENTS

ACKNOWLEDGMENTS

It takes many people to make a book, and my gratitude for their help is abounding. First, I would like to thank my family. Thea (1941–2009) inspired this writing, and her memory sustained the writer. Our daughters also helped. Alyda and Coleen helped with the various health complications that arose during the writing, and Coleen, who saw the book progressing each day, wondered if it would ever be done. Thea's and my granddaughters were also present at the birthing of this book. Maddi and Tori supported it by their visits, usually once a week, and Lexi, the oldest, read and commented on the manuscript in its later stages. Thank you all.

Two friends gave this an early read. Rebecca McClain read it many years ago before it really began to take shape. That was a heroic reading, truly an act of friendship. Zoe Cole also took an interest in the early versions of the manuscript.

My academic friends were all astonishing. I would like to make special mention of six of them in alphabetical order. None of them had the time to read and comment on yet another book, especially since they were all working on writing projects of their own in addition to their regular teaching and other duties. Still, they took the time to contribute to the book and to support me personally as the author.

David Jensen, the Academic Dean and Professor in the Clarence N. and Betty B. Frierson Distinguished Chair of Reformed Theology at Austin Presbyterian Theological Seminary, provided a careful and caring critique. He has always been sensitive to words and talks much about the "Word made flesh" as the source of and reason for theology.

Annette Mahoney, Professor of Psychology at Bowling Green State University, also puzzled over the manuscript. Her widely published research traces the positive and negative roles of religion and spirituality in the lives of individuals and families. Her articles and chapters have appeared in such publications as *The Oxford Handbook of Psychology and Spirituality* (2012).

Rebecca Nye is a child psychologist and Godly Play Trainer, as well as a researcher and consultant in the field of children's spirituality for schools, churches, hospitals, and academic institutions. She lives in Ely while teaching and supervising M.A. and Ph.D. students in various colleges in the Cambridge area. Rebecca wrote a detailed response to the book in November of 2014 as the book was beginning to take shape.

Timothy F. Sedgwick, the Clinton S. Quin Professor of Christian Ethics at Virginia Theological Seminary, sent seven pages of single-spaced comments in October of 2014. This made me take the book more seriously and guided its development.

Sam Wells, the vicar of St. Martin-in-the-Fields on Trafalgar Square and Visiting Professor of Christian Ethics at King's College, London, also read the manuscript. We had a long and animated discussion about the book over supper in London in the spring of 2015 when I was there to give some lectures.

Robert C. Whitaker, Professor in the Department of Public Health and Professor of Pediatrics at the Lewis Katz School of Medicine at Temple University in Philadelphia, not only read the manuscript in 2015 but he called me to talk about it at length. We have continued to discuss its implications for the shared work of theology and medicine concerning children's spirituality.

Thank you all.

My retreat for discussion about this manuscript and sometimes for solitary editing was the excellent, Italian restaurant in Denver called *Venice*. Thanks to you all, but especially to Alessandro Carollo, Chef-Owner; Christian Delle Fave, Executive Chef; Nunzio Marino, General Manager; and of course, Leticcia.

I would also like to express my gratitude to Davis Perkins, the publisher of CPI, and to Ryan Masteller, who produced the book.

The editor for this book was Dirk deVries. He has been a wellspring of encouragement, knowledge, practical experience, and the creative energy to keep the work moving in the right direction. We have worked together on various publishing projects for nearly fifteen years. This included working and celebration visits to Denver with Thea and Coleen. It was especially gratifying to me for him to be the editor for this particular book.

Ultimately, the responsibility for the book is mine and I happily accept that, but it gives me abiding pleasure to remember these wonderful people with gratitude.

Jerome W. Berryman
Denver, Colorado
February 4, 2016

Maturity beyond the Norm

This book invites sustained reflection on one of Jesus' most curious sayings. It is curious because it says that true maturity for adults, as part of God's kingdom, involves being like a child. We usually tell children to grow up, and we look down on adults who act like children, so this sounds as countercultural today as it was when Jesus first told it.

We will explore Jesus' saying by looking first at the child/ adult paradox, which is at the heart of his aphorism. The next four steps will discuss the literal, figurative, mystical, and ethical interpretations of his saying. To conclude we will make a soft closure that invites further reflection.

As the book developed over the years, it took a classical shape. I had to laugh when the four-fold way of biblical interpretation emerged. I had never taken this seriously as a theology student, well over fifty years ago, except as a bit of history, but there it was! This is why I used the *quadriga* to organize the book.

A *quadriga* was a Roman chariot drawn by four horses, harnessed abreast. The four horses symbolized the literal, figurative, mystical, and ethical approaches to scripture. My interpretation, however, began with the core paradox at the heart of Jesus' saying, so I added the chariot itself to the image, because it is suspended between its wheels, like a paradox is suspended between the two horns of its dilemma. The art response at the end of the book extends the image further. It became the charioteer, who gathers up the book's meaning to guide the *quadriga* home without getting stuck in either rigidity or chaos. The four-fold way became a six-fold way for reflecting on Jesus' saying.

A second kind of structure is the nesting of references to the creative process at different scales, like Russian dolls, throughout the book. Sometimes these references are implied, as in the overall organization of the book, and sometimes they are explicit. The creative process involves opening, scanning, insight, development, and a soft closure (avoiding both rigidity and chaos). The nesting of the creative process in the book's structure suggests how creativity appears in different scales throughout God's creation, and urges that for optimum development we need to align ourselves with the deep current of creativity that flows out from and returns to God.

The book also integrates several different kinds of theological language to explore Jesus' aphorism. Hans Frei (1922–1988) was so dissatisfied by people superficially dividing theology into liberal and conservative camps that he developed a more appropriate, five-part classification, based on the use of language, which is still used today.[1] This book uses all five kinds of theological language identified by Frei, so let's take

---

1. Frei's typology replaced Hugh Ross Mackintosh's *Types of Modern Theology*, which was still used in Protestant theological seminaries in the early 1960s. It divided Protestant theology into six types: feeling (Schleiermacher), "speculative rationalism" (Hegel), "moral values" (Albrecht Ritschl), "scientific religious history" (Troeltsch), the "theology of paradox" (Kierkegaard), and the "theology of the Word of God" (Barth).

David Ford, Regius Professor of Divinity at the University of Cambridge, included Frei's typology in his introduction to theology (Ford, *Theology: A Very Short Introduction* [Oxford, UK: Oxford University Press, 1999], 20–30). John R. Franke also used it in his "postconservative, Evangelical approach" to theology (Franke, *The Character of Theology: An Introduction to Its Nature, Task, and Purpose* [Grand Rapids, MI: Baker Academic, 2005], 30–35).

a moment now to examine Frei's classification system so we won't have to interrupt our discussion later to do so.

The first kind of theological language used speaks about God with words that are completely outside the domain of Christian language. Frei's example was Gordon Kaufman (1925–2011), who tried to remove all anthropomorphisms from his theology and favored philosophical and scientific language. In this spirit he referred to God as "serendipitous creativity." This approach to theology influenced chapter 4, where I discuss the mystical relationship with the Creator in terms of the creative process and fractals. Kaufman, who did not warm to mysticism, probably would not have approved of this, but I find it to be very helpful.

A second approach to theology mixes philosophical concerns with scripture, like the work of Rudolf Bultmann (1884–1976), who provided Frei's second example. This approach operates at the edge of Christian language. It avoids the cosmic mythology of the first century but still centers on the fundamental Christian experiences of existential anxiety, redemption, and especially in this book, the experience of God's creative force. This approach allows us to speak about the fundamental limits to our being and knowing, which create existential anxiety, an experience we have in common with people in the first century, even if they would not have used such language to describe it. We also share with them how Christian language—parables, sacred stories, liturgical action, and contemplative silence—can reveal God's loving presence to help cope with our mortal limits. This approach is used in chapter 3, especially in the discussion of anxiety and how Christian language and community can help cope with it.

Frei used Paul Tillich (1886–1965) to illustrate a third theological type. This approach responds to the questions posed by culture about life and death with responses from within the Christian language system. Chapter 3 shows how "The Parable of the Leaven" responds to questions children bring with them about life and death as they wonder together about the parable. The whole book, however, is a response to our culture's questions about maturity. It says how living in God's kingdom is a kind of maturity that goes beyond chronological age and cultural norms.

The fourth type of theological language used in this book is like that of Karl Barth, another example used by Frei. This kind of theological discussion stands almost entirely within the domain of Christian language. It is as if Christ-centered language were thrown like a lovely stone into the pool of our consciousness. The splash makes ripples of meaning that widen out in concentric circles from the Incarnation. This approach is especially useful when considering the church as a creative community. Barth stood within the circle of scripture and looked out at the world, including children, from that reference point, refusing to allow outside influences to re-define this view of the world. Barth's approach was used in chapter 4, where creativity and the church are connected by worship.

Frei used D. Z. Phillips to demonstrate a fifth use of theological language, which is at the opposite end of the spectrum from Kaufman. Phillips, following Wittgenstein, argued to keep the Christian language domain clear and distinct. This is because the meaning of words comes from their use in a particular language game. To mix domains would be like trying to play tennis with a football. This is why the Christian language game needs to be taught to children early and as a whole system, rather than as unrelated bits and pieces. When this language game is taught and spoken fluently with love, it becomes the language of love. This enables us, as John wrote in his first letter, to love not just in "word or speech, but in truth and action" (1 John 3:18).

The structure of the book—the *quadriga*, the nesting of the creative process like Russian dolls, and the use of five types of theological language—may seem unduly complex, but I don't think this structure will intrude on the book's flow. These are merely matters we need to discuss now, as I said above, so their explanation won't intrude later.

Finally, this book stands alone, but it also completes a line of thinking that began when Sam Keen, Jim Fowler, and I published *Life Maps* in 1978. This laid the groundwork for my approach to the spiritual guidance of children, which was described in *Godly Play* in 1991. *Teaching Godly Play* was published in 1995 with a much-improved second edition in 2009, and the eight volumes of *The Complete Guide to Godly Play* appeared from 2002 to 2012. The theological background for this approach to learning the art of making existential meaning with Christian language was explored in *Children and the Theologians* in 2009. The history, nature, and development of Godly Play were explored in *The Spiritual Guidance of Children* in 2013. In the same year Brendan Hyde published *The Search for a Theology of Childhood: Essays by Jerome W. Berryman from 1978–2009*. The book introduced here explores the kind of maturity Godly Play seeks for children and adults, but it is also based on what has been discovered through the use of Godly Play, which began as a question in 1960 when I began my formal theological training at Princeton Theological Seminary.

CHAPTER 1

Happiness and Maturity beyond the Norm

THE CHILD/ADULT PARADOX

The lure of lasting happiness is unshakable. Even when we are happy, we seek it. It is usually connected to maturity, which is more mundane, but it takes maturity to know the difference between authentic and frivolous happiness. More of the wrong kind of happiness is not always better—and sometimes it is much worse—so maturity is important when we seek lasting happiness.

When we look for maturity in the norms of society, we sometimes misinterpret or fail to learn from them. They also change. Steven Mintz addressed the changing views of maturity in *The Prime of Life: A History of Modern Adulthood*. Today's definition "took shape in the nineteenth century and reached its culmination in the 1950s. It then broke down in the early

1960s and shifted to a more diverse and individualistic conception . . . ," which we are still adjusting to.[1]

During this uncertain time we need a "new idea" to challenge our culture's mix of alternatives. There is no shortage of advice from the psychologists of happiness and from the happiness industry that is ready to sell us happiness at any cost (to us). I would rather talk about a different kind of idea that is curious in three ways. It is curious because it is odd and so old that it seems new. It is also curious because it involves our curiosity to make it work.

The "new" idea is to become like a child to be mature. The original speaker of this saying was clearly talking about optimum human development, but he put it in a way that seems strange to us. He talked about becoming part of "God's kingdom," which is a "place" that is both a state of mind and a way of life beyond society's changing norms. That is where, he implied, lasting happiness can be found.

This is a quirky and complex way of speaking, but that is how Jesus talked.[2] We don't have time for such talk, but that is nothing new. Christian theologians across the centuries did not take Jesus' aphorism very seriously either. They are more interested in children today,[3] but children are still overlooked as clues for authentic maturity. Jesus' saying is as counter cultural and counterintuitive today, as it was when he uttered it. This is why we need to explore it with care. How shall we proceed?

---

1. Steven Mintz, *The Prime of Life: A History of Modern Adulthood* (Cambridge, MA: Harvard University Press, 2015), x.

2. Jesus is reported to have said that children are at home where God reigns (Matthew 19:13–15, Mark 10:13–16, and Luke 18:15–17). We need to welcome them to know them, and when we know them, they can show us what we need to be like to live in God's dwelling place. Welcoming children and knowing them also makes Jesus and the one who sent him better known (Matthew 18:5, Mark 9:37, Luke 9:48). If we become like children, we can enter (Matthew 18:3), receive (Mark 10:15, Luke 18:17), and/or be born into (John 3: 3, 7) *God's kingdom.*

3. An example of this increased theological interest, involving six contemporary theologians, is discussed in chapter 7 of Jerome W. Berryman, *Children and the Theologians: Clearing the Way for Grace* (New York: Morehouse Publishing, 2009), 167–196.

THE PLAN FOR THE BOOK

We will begin by exploring the child/adult paradox, which is at the heart of Jesus' saying. It challenges us to be fully adult and fully children at the same time. In the second chapter we will think through what the child is like whom *we are to be like* to enter God's kingdom. We will consult theologians, historians of childhood, child psychologists, and our own memories of childhood to discover this. Chapter 3 takes the opposite approach. It invites us to expand our view of children by imagining them as parables of action. Textual children from the Gospels and living children from Houston will expand our view of their theological intuition. Chapter 4 discusses the nature of the creative process and how it runs all through God's creation. This is why we need to align our deep identity as creators with God's creativity to become mature beyond the norm. Unfortunately this alignment is often frustrated, which brings us to chapter 5. It discusses how our lives can flow in the deep channel of creativity, which is our home, despite the obvious decay and obfuscation of our fundamental identity as creators. The final chapter makes a soft closure that invites further integration and wonder about the book as a whole. It will take the form of an imaginative extension of Jesus' aphorism into a fable.

You may already have noticed that the four middle chapters of the book interpret Jesus' aphorism in a literal, figurative, mystical, and ethical way. This organization approximates the classical four-fold method used by early and medieval Christian theologians to interpret scripture. The four-fold way was sometimes called the *quadriga* because it is like a Roman chariot pulled by four horses harnessed abreast.

I have added two more perspectives to the classical view. As already mentioned, we will begin with the paradox at the heart of Jesus' aphorism. The chariot represents this paradox.

It is suspended between its two wheels, like the meaning of a paradox is suspended between the horns of its dilemma. The last chapter adds a sixth perspective, which is represented by the charioteer. It gathers up the themes in the book and invites further integration and reflection on them to guide the chariot home. As you can see, there are six chapters, one for each perspective.

I did not set out to use the *quadriga* to organize the book, but when I noticed that the emerging argument resembled it, I made the connection more explicit and found it helpful. This was a surprise! I had considered the fourfold approach to be interesting as ancient history but irrelevant for real use. It is seldom used today, so I was astonished to discover in 2014 that Karlfried Froehlich's *Sensing the Scriptures: Aminadab's Chariot and the Predicament of Biblical Interpretation* had revisited this tradition.[4]

---

4. Karlfried Froehlich, with the collaboration of Mark S. Burrows, *Sensing the Scriptures: Aminadab's Chariot and the Predicament of Biblical Interpretation* (Grand Rapids, MI: Wm. B. Eerdmans Publishing Co., 2014).

Froehlich's book was based on his 1997 Warfield Lectures at Princeton Theological Seminary and is full of the detail and depth one might expect from a brilliant scholar who spent his life studying the history of biblical interpretation. He found an image of Aminadab's Chariot in a stained-glass window in Abbot Suger's ambulatory of Saint-Denis in Paris (viii, 11–12, 140), but his book was organized around the mixed metaphor of Aminadab's Chariot with four horses and "one of the earliest allegorical poems in the Middle Ages" in which Alan of Lille described a chariot with five horses, one for each of the senses, with Reason as the charioteer.

The name "Aminadab" comes from Song of Solomon (Song of Songs) 6:12. The Latin Vulgate translated the obscure Hebrew *markevot ammi-nadib* as the name Aminadab to identify the chariots. A better translation is probably "chariots of my people."

Luther and other Protestant reformers condemned the four-fold way in favor of the literal view. William Tyndale (c. 1494–1536) attacked the four-fold way as a deception of the Pope and advocated for the plain sense of scripture (126). This negative view has survived to the present time. Froehlich wrote, "The gut feeling among us still is that allegory in biblical interpretation has been duly tried, convicted, sentenced and hanged, and that it remains only as an object of scorn and horror" (59). Still, much like Luther and Tyndale, who took delight in biblical metaphors and their usefulness for the spiritual life, Froehlich acknowledged that the imagination is always important for biblical interpretation (7).

THE TEXT OF THE APHORISM

Before we begin to explore Jesus' saying, let's take a good look at the texts on which it is based. Four of the sources are from the Gospels, and a fifth variation is from the non-canonical Gospel of Thomas. Here are the clusters of relevant references to bring Jesus' aphorism to life:

Matthew

"Truly I tell you, unless you change and become like children, you will never enter the kingdom of heaven. Whoever becomes humble like this child is the greatest in the kingdom of heaven. Whoever welcomes one such child in my name welcomes me." (Matthew 18:3–5)

Mark

"Whoever welcomes one such child in my name welcomes me, and whoever welcomes me welcomes not me but the one who sent me." (Mark 9:37)

"Truly I tell you, whoever does not receive the kingdom of God as a little child will never enter it." (Mark 10:15)

Luke

"Whoever welcomes this child in my name welcomes me, and whoever welcomes me welcomes the one who sent me; for the least among all of you is the greatest." (Luke 9:48)

"Truly I tell you, whoever does not receive the kingdom of God as a little child will never enter it." (Luke 18:17)

John

"Very truly, I tell you, no one can see the kingdom of God without being born from above." Nicodemus said to him, "How can anyone be born after having grown old? Can one enter a second time into the mother's womb and be born?" (John 3:3–4)

Gospel of Thomas

Jesus saw some infants at the breast. He said to his disciples: "These little ones are like those who enter the kingdom." (Logion 22)

As you can see, Jesus did not say that adults should pretend to be children while in reality remaining adults. We can't help but remain adults, when we become like children, which complicates things and makes the child/adult paradox as perplexing as it is fundamental to Jesus' saying.

It is naïve to think we can step outside our accumulated years and experience. It is also dangerous as well as irresponsible for an adult to become a child. This is what makes Jesus' paradox so curious, doubtful, and challenging. It invites us to increase the intensity of being truly children *as well as adults* to be mature beyond the norm. Anything less than both is hypocrisy, and Jesus did not like hypocrisy in any form. He called hypocrites "white-washed tombs," beautiful and white on the outside but dark and full of decay on the inside (Matthew 23:27). Authentic child/adult maturity, then, is not a dichotomy of pretense. It is a paradoxical "state," which is both a way of being in the world and a kind of consciousness of *God's* kingdom. It is a place, both personal and political, where one's maturity is not limited by cultural norms or chronological age.

THE HORNS OF THE PARADOX

The horns of Jesus' paradox are the kingdom-adult and the kingdom-child. We are to be both, through and through, so the paradox can't be managed by tearing the horns apart to look at them independently (and kill the bull) or leaping through the horns and somersaulting off the bull's back, like in old Crete. Singing the bull to sleep with our eloquence or avoiding the arena for contests with bulls won't work either, since we need to live the paradox. The child/adult paradox is a challenge, but it is even more complicated than it looks. This is because of the kind of language Jesus used to set it up.

Norman Perrin (1920–1976), a biblical scholar at the Divinity School of the University of Chicago, was one of the first to realize that Jesus used "kingdom" as a symbol (standing for something else) and "child" as a metaphor (signifying a likeness in unlikes). Both kinds of language "resist translation into another mode of discourse."[5]

Jesus' aphorism asks us to do the work needed to be open to God's presence as it is conveyed in a symbol (kingdom) and a metaphor (child) to us by his carefully chosen words. He was trying to involve the whole person—the knowing of the body by the senses, the knowing of the mind by reason, and the knowing of the spirit by contemplation—for us to live this paradox. He wanted us to move from logic to narrative. His goal was to change lives, not win arguments.

The symbol "kingdom" stands for God's mighty acts, such as the Exodus, which displayed a power that was overwhelming and unfathomable. The highest concentration of power known in the ancient world outside of nature was a "king," so this word was used to suggest the power in *God's* kingdom, a power that put earthly monarchs in an ultimate perspective. They ruled on behalf of God. Nebuchadnezzar, who thought

---

5. Norman Perrin, *Jesus and the Language of the Kingdom: Symbol and Metaphor in New Testament Interpretation* (Philadelphia: Fortress Press, 1976), 56.

he was all-powerful like God, went insane and ate grass in the fields like an ox until he came to his senses (Daniel 4:28–37).

When God reigns in one's life and in society, a transcendent energy is felt that demands the highest standard of personal and social justice, going beyond the practicalities and concerns of the cultural norm. God is eternal, so God's kingdom is also eternal, but Jesus prayed for this unlimited, heavenly reality to come on earth, to our time-bound and imperfect world. He was not more specific about how and when, because he was more interested in embodying God's kingdom to communicate its reality and helping people *prepare* for living in it than in formulating or discussing abstract definitions about it or speculating about when it might actually arrive.

The power of God's kingdom was associated with the creative process, which is how one can arrive at personal and social justice. We know the creative process was involved, because Jesus talked about the kingdom in terms of creative action—seeds *scattered* in different kinds of soil, weeds *sorted* after the harvest, the tiniest of all the seeds *growing* into the largest of the shrubs, leaven irresistibly *leavening* dough, a treasure *hidden and found* in a field, a merchant *searching for, finding, and selling everything* for the great pearl, and *pulling in* a net full of fish *to be sorted out* as good and bad afterward. This seems clear enough, but what isn't clear is why this kingdom of creating, known in the kingdom parables, had no king. Was creating itself the highest power?

The scattering, sorting, growing, leavening, hiding and finding, searching, pulling in and sorting out discloses a Creator who is known in creating instead of by being ruled with majesty and absolute authority from a distance. When Jesus prayed, he invited us to join him in prayer to "*our* Father"—ours as well as his. As one's father and mother create offspring, so does the Creator, and we are part of that great family.

Jesus inferred that rule in the kingdom is more like that of the father of a family in the Galilean countryside than the rule of Herod's sons or the *imperium* (power to command) of the Roman Caesar and his representatives. Jesus' heavenly father was a forgiving one, like fathers working closely and personally with their families in the fields, markets, carpenter shops, sheepfolds, barns, and perhaps nearby construction sites such as in Sepphoris, near where Jesus grew up. Galilean fathers were clearly in charge, but they did not rule impersonally from a distance like the royalty at the center of power in Jerusalem or Rome. The father and the mother of the family worked together, each with a role, to create together biologically, personally, and socially, like the parables suggested. Was this inference factually true or an idealization?

Eastern Mediterranean families in the first century, like every century, were complex in their own way. They often included several generations as well as slaves. The father ruled—whether Roman, Greek, or Jewish. He was responsible for the security and continuity of the family and sometimes "abused," as we think of it today, the women, children, and slaves by his exercise of power.[6] Crossan and others have argued that the kingdom Jesus talked about was "contrary to Mediterranean and indeed most human familial reality."[7] This

---

6. By the latter part of the first century, Christian families gathered to listen to the reading or reciting of Paul's letters and the Gospels in house churches. These texts were transforming when recited or read to "children, slaves, masters, or parents," because they talked about a new and complex family *related to God* instead of merely to the father, as ruler of the household. This was the primary way the new identity of Christians was formed. Margaret Y. MacDonald, *The Power of Children: The Construction of Christian Families in the Greco-Roman World* (Waco, TX: Baylor University Press, 2014), 71.

7. John Dominic Crossan, *Jesus: A Revolutionary Biography* (New York: HarperSan-Francisco, 1994), 60.

means that God's reign went beyond the normal, cultural view of maturity, then as well as now. This is why discussing the sociology of the Eastern Mediterranean in the first century can only carry us part way toward understanding the kingdom. We need to think theologically as well as historically[8] to understand that Jesus meant something outside the norm for the culture, his or ours, when he talked about the kingdom.

The distinction between theological thinking and historical thinking is an important one. A dramatic example involves Johannes Weiss (1863–1914) and Albrecht Ritschl (1822–1889). Weiss was a pupil and the son-in-law of Ritschl, who was, perhaps, the leading German theologian of his time. Ritschl thought that the kingdom would be ushered in by the ethical work of loving Christians around the world inspired by God, who is love. Weiss, on the other hand, published his concise, first edition of *Jesus' Proclamation of the Kingdom of God* in 1892. He argued that historically the kingdom was "the breaking out of an overpowering divine storm which erupts into history to destroy and to renew . . . and which man can neither further nor influence."[9] History contradicted theology in the same family.[10]

---

8. Jesus' upbringing may not have been as limiting as is sometimes thought. Geza Vermes notes that there is a metaphorical use of "carpenter" in Jewish writings in Aramaic (*naggar*), which suggests the connotation of "a 'scholar' or 'learned man.'" Geza Vermes, *Jesus the Jew: A Historian's Reading of the Gospels* (Philadelphia: Fortress Press, 1973), 21.

9. Quoted in Perrin, *Jesus and the Kingdom*, 67. Perrin tells this story respectfully and with perspective.

10. The first sentence in the later and larger 1900 edition of *Predigt Jesu* attempted a compromise. It read:

> As a pupil of Albrecht Ritschl I learned the importance of the idea of the Kingdom of God, which is the center of his theology; and I am still of the opinion that Ritschl's system, especially this central idea, is, when properly understood, the most suitable to awaken and sustain for our generation the sound and healthy religious life that we need. But I have long been troubled with a conviction that Ritschl's idea of the Kingdom of God and "the Kingdom of God" in the Message of Jesus are two very different things.

Note that the 1892 edition had 68 pages but the 1900 edition had 214 pages.

The life of Albert Schweitzer (1875–1965) shows this con-tradiction in a single person. He popularized Weiss' view of the kingdom with a long review and critique of the quest for the historical Jesus, but he observed that the Jesus revealed by the historians cannot bring Jesus "straight into our time as a Teacher and Saviour." The Jesus "that means something to our world" is a "mighty spiritual force." The method of history can-not "call spiritual life into existence."[11] It tells us about the past.

After clarifying the history versus theology distinction for himself, as well as others, Schweitzer entered medical school in 1905 at the age of thirty. After graduation he moved to Africa in 1913 to be a medical missionary most of the rest of his life. He embodied the "mighty spiritual force," whatever one might think today about the limitations of his colonial frame of mind during the early part of the last century.

Both theological and the historical interpretations of Jesus' saying are needed, because the theologian and historian have different methods and goals. This book is informed by histori-cal criticism, but its primary emphasis is on how the child/adult paradox might change lives by God's "mighty spiritual force."

We have now examined the kingdom-adult horn of the child/adult paradox. This brings us to the other horn, the kingdom-child. The kingdom-child is related to the symbol of the kingdom by contradicting the kingly meaning for maturity. The child metaphor carries God's more quiet, indirect, and cre-ative power on its back, like the donkey that carried Jesus into Jerusalem for the last time (Matthew 21:7: Mark 11:7; Luke 19:35; John 12:14; Zechariah 9:9). A king on a donkey is as startling as a child leading an adult into God's kingdom. The metaphor of the kingdom-child asks us what the likeness is in

---

11. Albert Schweitzer, *The Quest of the Historical Jesus* (New York: The Macmillan Company, 1964), 399.

the unlikeness of the child and the adult. This juxtaposition is meant to give rise to thought.

When we focus on the child aspect of the child/adult paradox, the kingdom-adult drops into a subsidiary role but remains in play. When people focus only on the ideal child, they often urge us to become more humble, wondering, trusting, innocent, playful, in touch with our bodies, and laughing to be mature.[12] This is a theological view. It is true, but it is only part of the story for this horn of the child/adult paradox.

People who stress the historical interpretation of the child metaphor sometimes take an opposite view to the ideal child. They stress that Jesus' saying was not about imitating the nature of children to enter the kingdom. It is about God's nature, not the child's.[13] When the child enters the kingdom it means that God invites everyone, *even children*. This infers rather negatively that if the kingdom includes children it must include *everyone* because children don't count for much. Dominic Crossan suggested something like this in *The Historical Jesus* (1993) and put it memorably in *Jesus: A Revolutionary Biography* (1994) when he said that the kingdom was and is a gathering of "nobodies" and "undesirables."

---

12. Two examples will be given. The first is a book by a Roman Catholic, who was influenced by Jung. She talks about getting in touch with the Christ child and the other participants in the nativity scene found in Matthew and Luke. It includes ways to cope with the "shadow child," who is destructive when repressed. The book ends with a beautiful meditation on Michelangelo's Pieta, which invites the reader to participate in the dying and rising child of Mary and God, the Father. This resource is: Jean Gill, *Unless You Become Like a Little Child* (New York: Paulist Press, 1985).

A second example is a book by a Presbyterian minister, Timothy J. Mooney. He dedicated his book to "restoring the awe, wonder, joy and resiliency of the human spirit." Like Gill's book, it provides spiritual practices to help the reader become more like a child. This resource is: Timothy J. Mooney, *Becoming Like a Child: Restoring the Awe, Wonder, Joy & Resiliency of the Human Spirit* (Woodstock, VT: Christian Journeys from Skylight Paths Publishing, 2014).

13. Hans-Ruedi Weber in *Jesus and the Children: Biblical Resources for Study and Preaching* (Geneva: World Council of Churches, 1979), 19.

It is astonishing how a word standing for something else (kingdom-adult) and a word that evokes a likeness in things that are unlike (kingdom-child) can come together in a paradox to invite one to enter, receive, and/or be born into God's kingdom. Jesus' art did this, but this art intentionally did not specify angelic or "nobody" children, nor did it say whether the power of the kingdom is the creative process. We have to work that out for ourselves. What Jesus did stress was that the child/adult paradox is at the heart of maturity beyond the norm.

PARADOX AND EVERYDAY REALITY

The word "paradox" comes from the Greeks. A *paradoxon* (Greek *para*, "against," and *doxa*, "opinion" or "expectation") is an ancient term, but we are confounded by paradoxes every day. Perhaps the best example is not from Greek philosophy but from one of the most important novels of the twentieth century, Joseph Heller's *Catch-22*.

"Catch-22" was an informal rule used to decide whether those flying combat missions during World War II were crazy and should be relieved of their duties. If flyers said they were crazy to get out of flying, they were considered sane, because flying the bombing missions was truly crazy.

The term "Catch-22" entered the English language as an insolvable logical puzzle, a paradox with existential implications. Captain John Yossarian, the B-25 bombardier who is the main character in Heller's story, expressed his admiration for the simplicity and inescapability of Catch-22 with "a respectful whistle." The only way out of the vicious paradox was humor, exaggeration, ridicule, and satire to expose its folly. The paradox in Jesus' saying also calls for "a respectful whistle," but its paradox is virtuous rather than vicious. It causes health rather than undermines it.

When Jesus healed a lame man, Luke wrote, as translated by de Lubac, "Today we have seen *paradoxa!*" (Luke 5:26). The Greek word was translated into the Latin of the Vulgate Bible by the word *mirabilia* (wonderful things). Henri de Lubac S.J. (1896–1991), who noted this in his *Paradoxes of Faith*, also observed that the function of paradox in the Christian language system is to invite wonder.

Henri de Lubac was a great Jesuit scholar who helped prepare the way for Vatican II. He interpreted the history of dogma as a series of paradoxes, such as the divinity-humanity paradox of Jesus' nature or the three-in-one nature of the Holy Trinity. Such contradictions are intended to invite deep reflection and emotional participation rather than dismissal as logical absurdities. Lubac wrote, "Paradox is the search or wait for synthesis. It is the provisional expression of a view which remains incomplete, but whose orientation is ever towards fullness."[14] Dogma needs to stay close to its paradoxical roots, because the wonder it arouses is only a few steps away from the mystery of God, who is always both hidden *and* revealed.[15] The paradox of *deus absconditus et praesens* invites us into the game of hide

---

14. Henri de Lubac, *Paradoxes of Faith* (San Francisco: Ignatius Press, 1987), 9.

15. Two passages that refer specifically to children are Deuteronomy 29:29 ("The secret things belong to the Lord our God, but the revealed things belong to us and to our children forever, to observe all the words of this law.") and Matthew 11:25–26 ("At that time Jesus said, 'I thank you, Father, Lord of heaven and earth, because you have hidden these things from the wise and the intelligent and have revealed them to infants; yes, Father, for such was your gracious will.'"). There are many more places in the Hebrew and Christian scriptures where God is referred to as hidden and revealed.

Paul Tillich wrote in the "Foreword" to John Dillenberger's *God Hidden and Revealed* (Philadelphia: Muhlenberg Press, 1953): "As is evident in this book, there is no necessary conflict between these two interpretations. He who is hidden as the abyss behind everything manifest reveals himself in contrast to everything man can expect."

and seek with God, which adds the time and space of narrative to the paradox of God's nature.

Knowing God can't help but be a mysterious paradox. For example, when you focus on the experience of one person of the Trinity, the other two become subsidiary and yet are still active in the relationship.[16] Michael Polanyi (1891–1976) described this aspect of knowing as focal (explicit and conscious) and tacit (implicit and subsidiary) in his *Personal Knowledge* (1958). He was primarily concerned with trying to portray how science is actually practiced, but his focal-subsidiary distinction also pertains to knowing God and everyday events such as riding a bicycle. Bike riding requires *at the same time* the coordination of the riding's subsidiary mechanics to make the bicycle go, with the focus on the destination to get where you intend. As Lubac wrote, "paradox exists everywhere in reality, before existing in thought. Paradox, in the best sense, is objectivity."[17] It was *this sense* of "objectivity" that Polanyi made clearer for scientific, theological, and everyday knowing.

When theology is domesticated, as in manuals and textbooks, it is shorn of its subsidiary knowing. Listing only explicit, conscious, theological conclusions blinds us to subsidiary

---

16. Dante also expressed this double aspect of knowing with the griffin that brought Beatrice's chariot from heaven at the end of *Purgatorio*. When Dante looked into her eyes, he saw that when she looked at the griffin she did not see it as a blend of the head of an eagle and the body of a lion. She saw the united power of both without any mixing. She saw each whole, back and forth. Dante said this was like tasting food, which satisfies and yet makes one hungry (XXXI, 115–129, *Pergatorio*). Dante may have been also suggesting this is how we ought to see the Incarnation.

Charles S. Singleton translated this complexity as "the twofold animal gleaming therewithin, now the one, now with the other bearing" *("con altri, con altri reggimenti")*. Dante Alighieri, *The Divine Comedy: Pergatorio*, translated Charles S. Singleton (Princeton, NJ: Princeton University Press, 1973), 346–349.

17. de Lubac, *Paradoxes of Faith*, 10.

knowing, which is where the original mystery is. An existential paradox, such as being born to die, demands the involvement of the whole person, consciously and unconsciously, to know and cope with the reality it expresses, because it is our wholeness that is at risk in the reality of the paradox. Jesus' saying, therefore, profoundly invites rather than stifles the participation of the whole person to become part of the kingdom through the child/adult paradox.

The church has always been careful about its language. Sometimes this has led to obsessive and violent action. People in past centuries were tortured and burned at the stake for "errors" in their language, written or spoken. Even in the twentieth century, important theologians, such as Teilhard de Chardin, were "silenced" and forbidden to publish, because of their "mistakes." We will return to Teilhard de Chardin in chapter 4, but what needs to be said now is that the history of heresy is the opposite of the history of dogma in Lubac's sense.

Heresy is the story of lost paradoxes and the loss of a sense of humor in the church. The debates about Christology have been especially intense and sometimes violent, because keeping the paradoxical truth of Christ's nature whole always struggles against one-sided, reductive interpretations such as "Christ was only a man" or "Christ was pure divinity." The paradoxical mystery of Christ's nature cannot be experienced by force of arms or by logical reduction. It takes openness and personal courage to live fully into the paradox and to turn it into your story. The same is true of the child/adult paradox.

Laughter lives next door to paradox, because the involvement that the paradox invites is not cut and dried. It is playful. There may even have been a touch of humor intended in the creation of some of the classical Greek paradoxes. The liar's paradox is an example. To say, "This statement is a lie," does not involve us existentially. Its superficial cleverness does not deserve a soft whistle like Catch-22, but it does deserve a wink or slight smile. It shows how language can be used to chase its tail, like a kitten, as well as to state profound meaning in paradoxes to point "objectively," in de Lubac's sense, toward fundamental, living reality.

Jesus' play with language provoked the imagination of his listeners to see things from an eternal perspective, which got him and his followers into grave trouble. The result of this "trouble," however, enabled Jesus to enact yet another paradox, Holy Week/Easter, to teach us more than we could otherwise imagine about the implications of being born to die and the quintessential Christian emotion of joy, which we will come to as the book unfolds.

Jesus' playfulness with life and language included his refusal to think about adults and children in a "normal" way. He did not use "children" as an illustration for immaturity, like Paul did.[18] This refusal, if noticed, must have surprised some, but when he named children as the ultimate guides for showing adults the kingdom, the surprise may have turned to perplexity or even anger. The threat of Jesus' challenge has quieted down over the centuries from familiarity. Today his becoming-like-a-child aphorism is usually met with indifference, which is less profound but much harder to deal with as a response than anger. Anger, at least, is engaged.

The child/adult paradox invites deep engagement. When the invitation is accepted a multitude of related paradoxes

---

18. Paul's use of children as an illustration for immaturity may be found in I Corinthians 13:11, where we are told to put away childish things to be mature. With more nuance I Corinthians 14:20 tells us to not be children in our *thinking* but innocent as children with regards to evil. In Ephesians 4:14 we are told to be no longer like children, tossed to and fro by every "wind of doctrine."

are stirred up. Sometimes aphorisms stand independently and other times they sum up a tradition, but they also link to other sayings in loose, expanding networks of meaning. Jesus' aphorism is as weighty as a book, because it stands in the midst of many relationships, which link the themes of children, adults, maturity, and God's kingdom.[19] This enchanted web will lead us beyond the aphorism later in the book to find its larger meaning, but for now let's follow it into a network of additional paradoxes.

The network of paradoxes evoked by Jesus' aphorism includes the contradiction between creating (children) versus conserving (adults). A second paradox stimulated by the aphorism involves the global learning of children in tension with the focused learning of adults. A third paradox aroused is that we are born (children) to die (adults).

Jesus' aphorism also suggests that becoming is *permanent*, like during childhood, rather than becoming-to-be in a permanent state of adult maturity. This shatters the hope of entering a state of perfection, which was longed for in ancient times and by all of us at some time. In contrast, Jesus said that life is neither just becoming nor just being. It is living in the continuing creativity of the kingdom, which flows out of the child/adult paradox.

There are many more associations. You can think of additional ones yourself, but I would like to mention one more. This is the paradox of good and evil. Good and evil have been related in three ways. Some, like Jean-Jacques Rousseau (1712–1778), say that we are born good and become

19. Some of this paragraph draws on John Dominic Crossan, *In Fragments: The Aphorisms of Jesus* (San Francisco: Harper and Row, 1983), 20. Crossan's "aphoristic model" was illustrated by interpreting Jesus' sayings concerning children and the kingdom (313–327).

evil because society corrupts our original innocence. Others, like St. Augustine (354–430), say that we are born evil and by God's grace can become good if chosen by God. Still others, like John Locke (1632–1704), consider that we are born neutral, so it is nurture, not our original nature that matters. We will return to this question, especially in chapter 5, but for now we can say that both nature and nurture are involved in the unstable mixture of good and evil that makes up our paradoxical nature.

In summary, then, when we experience the child/adult paradox, it stimulates a whole network of associated paradoxes such as creating/conserving, global knowing/focused knowing, birth/death, becoming/being, and good/evil that are all involved in optimum human development. Jesus didn't say this directly but implied it by stimulating a multi-layered network of paradoxes standing within the paradoxical Christian language domain.

HOW AND WHY THE APHORISM WORKS

There is little in our everyday understanding of maturity, as an accumulation of years and experience, to show us what God's kingdom is like. We know from the Lord's Prayer (Matthew 6:9–13; Luke 11:2–4) that God's kingdom comes on earth, but it comes *from* heaven, so our worldly customs are not decisive to define it. This is why Jesus tried to surprise us with his aphorism into reconsidering what optimum development might really be.

He did not counsel us to get in touch with our "inner child" or to cultivate the characteristics of the "ideal child" to be nicer adults. He did not urge us to consider how the child is "parent" to the adult, which in 1802 was insightful poetry by

Wordsworth but has since become a cliché.[20] Jesus' aphorism was much more complex than Wordsworth's "natural piety," which is still of interest today, as can be seen in the enthusiasm for such important publications as *The Oxford Handbook of Psychology and Spirituality* (2012).

As valid and important as the poetry and science of natural piety might be, Jesus did not tell us how he arrived at his aphorism's conclusion. He did not define the key terms he used: "children" and "kingdom." He ran no "objective" experiments and sent out no questionnaires. He did no statistical analysis. He did not even name cultural maturity as a necessary part of his aphorism, expecting us to understand that it is. What he did leave us with was a terse, forceful saying with a paradox buried deep in its center that we must work out and live for ourselves. Why?

No one—not even God—can find maturity *for us*. We must discover it for ourselves, or it won't be ours! This is why Jesus nudged us forward, contributing to God's grace with his aphorism, to help us discover maturity for our own lives. He suggested the meaning, made it intriguing, and then hid it, like a treasure in a field and invited us to come out into the fields to

---

20. Wordsworth's poem "My Heart Leaps Up" is also known as "The Rainbow" and was written on March 26, 1802:

My heart leaps up when I behold
A rainbow in the sky:
So was it when my life began;
So is it now I am a man;
So be it when I shall grow old,
Or let me die!
The Child is father of the Man;
And I could wish my days to be
Bound each to each by natural piety.

This crystallized Wordsworth's thought and launched his much longer "Ode: Intimations of Immortality," which he began to write the next day. We will return to the question of "natural piety" often in this book, sometimes implicitly and sometimes explicitly.

play and find it. He invited us to come out of the house of our everyday thinking to discover a maturity we cannot personally create in any other way than by our own discovery.

If you listen carefully in the open fields of play, you can hear the laughter in Jesus' aphorism, but his saying is not a joke, gag, prank, or quip. The laughter it evokes signals the delight of discovery rather than scorn or power. Jesus' aphorism does not put us down. It lifts us up with its laughter.

Entering the playing fields of meaning created by Jesus' aphorism is like joining a conversation already in progress. There is controversy because aphorisms sometimes contradict each other, like the sayings about fools in Proverbs (26:4–5). The writer, identified as Solomon, counsels us to not answer fools lest we become like them and (at the same time) to answer them so they won't become wise in their own eyes. The child/adult contradiction in Jesus' aphorism was even more compressed. It stands *within* the few words of his aphorism itself! It challenges our views of maturity, but welcomes us into the conversation with an open smile. An aphorism is not a law.

The use of aphorisms to create meaning has fallen onto hard times since the rise of science. This is ironic since Francis Bacon (1561–1626) was, perhaps, the most famous champion of aphorisms in the modern, English-speaking world.[21] The irony lies in the fact that in addition to being the Lord Chancellor of England, he was also a philosopher of science, who helped move Europe toward modern experimental science. His

---

21. Oscar Wilde was a master of epigrams, which are like aphorisms. He is probably the most quoted author in English after Shakespeare. An example of his epigrams is: "We are all in the gutter, but some of us are looking at the stars." The distinctions between wisecracks, epigrams, aphorisms, adages, and maxims is subtle and sometimes tortured. The differences are often rooted in different languages and cultures. These distinctions may be fine (in two senses) but in this book we are most interested in aphorisms and sayings, which are used as synonyms.

Novum Organum Scientiarum of 1620 (*The New Tool for Science*), which played a major part in this earthshaking shift, was written mostly in numbered aphorisms.

The title of Bacon's book implied his seventeenth century challenge to Aristotle's original *Organon*, written some two millennia earlier. Bacon advocated for a new logical tool, inductive reasoning with experimentation, to counter the exclusive use of deductive reasoning that Aristotle had discussed in his original *Organon* and which his *medieval interpreters* established as the gold standard for logic.

Bacon championed aphorisms because they compress vast amounts of knowledge into concise statements, which do not burden the reader with illustrations and extraneous thought. He also thought that a well-crafted aphorism stimulates thought. He and Jesus agreed on the art and value of such sayings, but Bacon used his aphorisms to challenge the closed-minded use of Aristotle's logic while Jesus challenged the customary view of maturity for his time and ours.

This brings us to the implied connection between happiness and maturity, which we introduced at the beginning of this chapter. It is now time to make that connection more explicit. We will use an experimental and rational point of view to do this. Bacon told an aphorism to advocate for using such a non-aphoristic strategy:

> "Those who have handled sciences have been either men of experiment or men of dogmas. The men of experiment are like the ant, they only collect and use; the reasoners resemble spiders, who make cobwebs out of their own substance. But the bee takes a middle course: It gathers its material from the flowers of the garden and of the field, but transforms and digests it by a power of its own. . . . Therefore from a closer

and purer league between these two faculties, the experimental and the rational . . . much may be hoped."[22]

HAPPINESS AND OPTIMUM DEVELOPMENT

Suppose you meet a friend and ask, "Hi, how's it going?"

"Well, my overall satisfaction with life is okay. I think my meaningfulness and sense of purpose is good, but I could really do with a bit more moment to moment experienced well-being."

"Right. I understand. I'm actually pretty happy with my experienced well-being. I just wish I had more overall satisfaction. What really bothers me though is when I think long term. I am unhappy with my sense of meaningfulness and purpose."

We can be happy or unhappy *with our happiness* and we can break it down into several kinds of sub-happiness. At least since Plato and Aristotle in the fourth and fifth centuries BCE, we humans in the West have explicitly connected happiness with a kind of maturity that involves living by four cardinal virtues (justice, prudence, courage, and moderation). These are not the only virtues, but they are the ones on which the others "hinge." The Latin *cardo* (door hinge) is the word that "cardinal" comes from. The same four virtues are also found in texts from The Apocryphal/Deuterocanonical Books of the Bible (Wisdom of Solomon 8:7 and 4 Maccabees 1:18–19).

Martin Seligman tells us that Americans value "self-esteem, good looks, assertiveness, autonomy, uniqueness, wealth, and competitiveness." These are virtues that most philosophers and theologians over the centuries in the West have found trivial if not dangerous for lasting happiness.

---

22. Francis Bacon, *Novum Organum Scientiarum*, Book I, Aphorism 95. The cover of his 1620 publication showed a ship with its sails full of wind passing through the Pillars of Hercules into the uncharted Atlantic from the well-mapped Mediterranean.

Seligman and a team of scholars found that "there are no less than six virtues that are endorsed across every major religious and cultural tradition."[23] They are: wisdom/knowledge, courage, love/humanity (in the sense of being *humane*), justice, temperance, and spirituality/transcendence. This list proved unworkable for the psychologists because, as Seligman said, they "want to build and measure these things." Their focus became the "routes" (behavior) by which one arrives at these end points and how to help people get there.

For our purposes the most striking result of this study was its general agreement with the philosophical and theological traditions in the West. In fact, Seligman's book about "authentic happiness" reminds one of natural philosophy before the seventeenth century when the transition began, to our present views of "science" and "religion," which has hardened into opposing systems of propositional statements.

Peter Harrison argued recently that before the seventeenth century the natural philosophy of the Greeks and then the Christians was "always pursued with moral and religious ends in mind." He wrote, "We know this because the relevant historical actors state it unambiguously."[24] We shall have more to say about Seligman's important contributions to the study of happiness in a moment.

The cardinal virtues are justice, prudence, courage, and moderation. Prudence enables us to find the golden mean in the other three, such as courage being neither timidity nor foolhardiness but responsible action in between that is appropriate

---

23. Martin E. P. Seligman, *Authentic Happiness: Using the New Positive Psychology to Realize Your Potential for Lasting Fulfillment* (New York: Simon & Schuster, Aria Paperback, 2002), 130.

24. Peter Harrison, *The Territories of Science and Religion* (Chicago: The University of Chicago Press, 1015), 52.

for the situation. In the thirteenth century St. Thomas Aquinas creatively summarized theology to add the three theological virtues—faith, hope, and love—to the four cardinal ones to give us seven virtues to guide our lives.

The cardinal virtues can be honed by awareness and effort, but the theological virtues are given by God's grace. God can love us and guide us into faith, hope, and love, but we cannot will them directly into reality. We can clench our fists and try with all our might, but faith, hope, and love are not fully under our control. They seem to emerge as a byproduct of the way we are in the world as part of some sort of larger creativity. What is clear, however, is that the good life, guided by the seven virtues, is what gives us authentic happiness. We will discuss this more in chapter 5, but for now let's look at current research about maturity and happiness to enrich our view about the connection between happiness and optimum development.

The longest and most developed longitudinal study of human development to date is the Grant Study, which primarily followed some 268 physically and mentally healthy college sophomores, starting with their undergraduate days in 1939 to 1944 at Harvard to their deaths. It was limited at first to males, but the study has implications for all of us, and related studies, added later, included women and men growing up in less-advantaged environments.

The Grant Study was somewhat unique for many years because of its "deep data." It involved statistics, questionnaires, personal interviews, and medical exams across the decades of the participants' lives, but the stories derived from this vast collection of information made it a living document. This combination of science and narrative was one of the many contributions of George Vaillant, who became director of the study in 1967 at about the age of thirty-three. He reported on the men up to the age of fifty-five in his *Adaptation to Life* (1977) and continued to report on them in *Aging Well* (2002). He concluded his reporting in *Triumphs of Experience* (2012). By the time *Triumphs* was published, the participants had lived into their nineties and Vaillant was a much changed psychiatrist in his late seventies.

The greatest impact on "life satisfaction" for this group was "warmth of relationships." This experience allowed some to recover from terrible childhoods, but a happy childhood was found to be a lifelong source of strength. Vaillant summed up the study in his mildly iconoclastic way. "Happiness is only the cart; love is the horse." He had learned, "There are two pillars of happiness revealed by the seventy-five-year-old Grant Study. One is love. The other is finding a way of coping with life that does not push love away."[25]

Psychology in general became interested in happiness during the 1990s. Vaillant and the Grant Study helped bring about this shift of interest from investigating how to heal what goes wrong to helping things go right. It became obvious that we are drawn by our future as much as driven by our past. Two leading examples of this movement are Martin Seligman, author of *Authentic Happiness*, and Mihaly Csikszentmihalyi, who wrote *Flow: The Psychology of Optimal Experience*. This approach has been called "positive psychology" and grew out of the earlier work of Abraham Maslow (1908–1970), Carl Rogers (1902–1987), and Eric Fromm (1900–1980).

Sonja Lyubomirsky, a professor at the University of California, Riverside, noted in *The How of Happiness* (2007) that happiness is about fifty percent a predisposition (genetically

---

25. George E. Vaillant, *Triumphs of Experience: The Men of the Harvard Grant Study* (Cambridge, MA: The Belknap Press of Harvard University Press, 2012), 50.

determined as based on twin studies), ten percent circumstances, and forty percent under our own control. Psychology's interest in happiness has brought the world of science into conversation with the classical interests of philosophy and theology concerning character and virtue.

The field of public policy also became interested in happiness to help formulate legislation. In 2013 the National Research Council of the National Academies[26] produced an impressive report called "Subjective Well-Being." It emphasized the difference between *evaluative* well-being (overall satisfaction with life) and *experienced* well-being (moment-by-moment feelings) and drew attention to a third measure called "*eudaimonic* well-being, which refers to a person's perceptions of meaningfulness, sense of purpose, and the value of his or her life."[27] These were the kinds of happiness illustrated in the dialogue at the beginning of this section.

The term "*eudaimonic* well-being" is redundant but helpful. It uses Plato's and Aristotle's Greek word, *eudaimonia*, which refers to a state of having a good indwelling spirit. This spirit involves a contented state of being healthy, happy, and prosperous. *Eudaimonia* is usually translated as "well-being" or "flourishing." Aristotle thought that human beings seek happiness as naturally as acorns grow into oaks, but it takes time to develop the prudence to balance the extremes we are sometimes drawn to in order to follow his golden mean.

---

26. The National Academies' mission is "to improve government decision making and public policy, increase public understanding, and promote the acquisition and dissemination of knowledge in matters involving science, engineering, technology, and health." It is funded by a mix of foundations, state governments, the private sector, and philanthropy. The first independent adviser for government in this area was established by congressional charter in 1863 and signed into law by President Lincoln.

27. Quoted in Cass R. Sunstein, "Who Knows If You're Happy?" *The New York Review*, December 4, 2014, 20–22.

Happiness also became a concern of economics. Daniel Kahneman is a long-time leader in this field. He is an Israeli-American psychologist and professor *emeritus* of psychology and public affairs at the Woodrow Wilson School in Princeton. Kahneman shared the 2002 Nobel Prize in Economic Sciences with Vernon L. Smith for what is called "behavioral economics." Behavioral economics argues that the assumed "rational agent" of traditional economics needs a broader definition because of the irrational ways we actually make decisions about risk.[28] We typically use a collection of "heuristics," which are shortcuts (like aphorisms) that can lead to errors based on "cognitive biases" that blind us to what is at stake.

Kahneman cautioned us to be wary of decision making exclusively by intuition (thinking quickly). This approach needs to be tempered by reining in our undue sense of confidence in heuristics by using formal, rational thought (thinking slowly). This is why we need to be careful about using aphorisms without sustained reflection, hence the rationale for this book which asks us to think carefully and slowly about Jesus' aphorism concerning optimum human development and happiness.

All of the above studies of happiness are about adults. Children's language skills and life experience don't yet allow them to make the kind of distinctions that adults make about their happiness. Six-year-olds don't talk like the people in the hypothetical conversation at the head of this section. There have been occasions, however, when adults have noticed that children can contribute to their understanding of happiness.

Martin Seligman wrote, "Authentic happiness comes from identifying and cultivating your most fundamental strengths

---

28. This critique is sometimes associated with contrasting an "Econ" to a "Human" by Thaler and Sunstein in their book *Nudge* (2008).

and using them every day in work, love, play, and parenting."[29] This kind of "authenticity" is adult, but when his five-year-old daughter Nikki decided on her fifth birthday that she was not going to whine anymore, he listened. She informed her father that if she could stop whining, he could stop being a grouch. He wrote, "In that moment, I resolved to change."[30]

A child had taught Seligman how to be more adult. Wise children teaching adults has often been commented on throughout the centuries. The old Romans had a word for such children. They called them a *puer senex*, an old child. Lisa Miller, a psychologist, included a section in *The Spiritual Child* called "Let's Go In!: Children Summon Us for a Sacred Journey."[31] Isaiah's understanding of how a little child will lead us into the Messianic Age (Isaiah 11:6) and Jesus' aphorism about children teaching us how to become part of God's kingdom join with the modern psychologists and ancient Romans to appreciate what children can teach adults about becoming like a child.

Children don't always teach adults about maturity and happiness in a direct and verbal way. They often teach nonverbally by being themselves. People who publish books about children's spirituality understand this. The covers they put on their books often display children's faces, showing the exuberant benefits of their spirituality.

Photographs of children's faces are prominent on the covers of *The Spirit of the Child* (2006) by David Hay with Rebecca Nye, *Children's Spirituality* (2009) by Rebecca Nye, *Through the Eyes of a Child* (2009) by Olive M. Fleming and Anne Richards, *The Spiritual Dimension of Childhood* (2008) by

---

29. Seligman, *Authentic Happiness*, xi.

30. Ibid., 28.

31. Lisa Miller, *The Spiritual Child: The New Science on Parenting for Health and Lifelong Thriving* (New York: St. Martin's Press, 2015), 46–50.

Brendan Hyde and Kate Adams, *Children's Spirituality: Searching for Meaning and Connections* (2008) by Brendan Hyde, and my own book, *The Spiritual Guidance of Children* (2013). Art portraying children's faces is also used on the cover of *The Child in Christian Thought* (2001) and *The Child in the Bible* (2008), edited and contributed to by Marcia Bunge.

The most recent visual argument for the health and happiness of children's spirituality was on the cover of Lisa Miller's *The Spiritual Child* (2015). The face of an exuberant, joyful child infers that, as Miller says, the reality of children's spirituality is "hardwired." Her book goes on to provide a literature review about the psychological reality of children's spirituality and its benefits for parents, along with advice for parents about how to support the spirituality of their children and adolescents.

Still, when we look carefully at individual children and read their nonverbal communication with care, it is sometimes hard to tell whether they are happy or not. We want to believe that children are happy all the time, like on the covers of books about their spirituality, but, like us, this is not always the case. Let's take a moment to meet two children who were neither happy nor models for entering God's kingdom. They raise important questions we need to discuss about Jesus' child/adult paradox as the key to maturity beyond the norm.

In 1963 my wife, Thea, and I became worried about a child at the Head Start program where Thea worked. Mary (not her real name) was five and had many physical and mental challenges. What worried us most was that she kept trying to torture and kill the animals in the classroom. We went to visit her at home.

At home Mary was the same angry, awkward, and out-of-control child she was at school. Her parents were exhausted.

The constant responsibility for their little girl's care had worn them out. Their sense of humor and creativity were threadbare. They were afraid to have more children because providing care for Mary was overwhelming.

The father, who was a welder, made Mary a steel bed with a top on it. They locked Mary in it at night to keep her safe and to protect them while they slept. They also built a strong, high fence around their yard, so Mary could go outside during the day without getting lost or injured . . . or injuring anyone else. They did not know what else to do.

Thea and I did not know what else to do, either. Mary's needs were endless, while anyone's ability to meet them was limited. The Head Start program had been a tremendous gift to this family. It gave the mother a moment to rest and regain her equilibrium during the week.

As we drove away from our visit, we had a much greater empathy and compassion for Mary *and* her parents than before we visited their home, but we too were overwhelmed. We were young parents with a little girl of our own and did not have the resources—emotionally, financially, or professionally—to help. All we could do was support the Head Start program, which we did. Our reasonable but inadequate response caused tears of frustration and sadness for many years. Now, over fifty years later, I can still see Mary vividly.

Mary did not have many advantages, but Matt (not his real name) did. His mom was a famous child psychologist. She traveled all over the world to lecture about children. Her seven-year-old Matt was a bright but troubled child. Soon after we moved next door, he began to break into our house to steal inconsequential things. We became increasingly uneasy about finding him wandering around our house when we returned home, but what really scared us was his love of killing frogs.

I often found Matt at the small stream between our two houses. His eyes were shining and his laughter chaotic, as he smashed little frogs to bits with big rocks. Again, we were overwhelmed by the situation. All we could think of doing was to ask Matt's mother to keep him on their side of the stream. She did her best. A year later we moved to another city and, as with Mary, we lost touch, but we never forgot Matt or Mary.

Are these two children good guides for us to follow to be part of God's kingdom? Yes and no . . . Once Thea and I welcomed Mary and Matt, we learned from them consciously and unconsciously about this additional complexity to the child/adult paradox. We were unable to change them, but they changed us. Did they show us how to be part of the kingdom by their overwhelming needs and unhappiness? Perhaps.

What I do know is that welcoming children is not just about being nice to nice children. All children need firm but kind limits, but some have so many needs that they can easily consume all our energy and creativity when we try to guide them. This is why needy children require a whole network of people to love them and to cope in practical ways with their unlimited needs. In personal terms, Mary and Matt guided Thea and me toward working with children the rest of our lives—all kinds of children. They were not the models for but the means for this vocation.

Mary and Matt also introduced us to the depth of the reality that children are not always happy. They have the same existential anxieties we adults have, and at times this anxiety can be overwhelming. Mary and Matt were angry and violent in their unhappiness, but all children express their pain and anxiety in ways that shout to adults if we have the ears to hear them. They fuss and weep for no apparent reason. They get moody and go off by themselves. They become obsessed with video games and other things to distract themselves from their pain and meaninglessness. They go to the hospital to heal and become lethargic instead of actively cooperating. Don't we adults do the same?

The connection between optimum development and happiness is not just an adult phenomenon as most of the studies in this section imply. We need to resist being blinded by such studies to the reality of children, because if we become blind to them we will never be able to think slowly and carefully about Jesus' aphorism and the child/adult paradox at its heart. This in turn will prevent us from finding clues for seeking maturity beyond the norm in children as well as ourselves.

CONCLUSION

Jesus' saying was brief and to the point, but the point is a paradox, so it resists reduction and invites living. We sometimes try to break paradoxes into pieces to reduce their meaning to one or the other horn of the dilemma, but in this chapter we have tried to resist that. In future chapters we will take the paradox apart, but we needed to begin here, as you can see, with the exuberant challenge of the child/adult paradox.

This chapter has said that to be part of God's kingdom we need to live out the child/adult paradox from logic to narrative. We need to be fully a child and fully an adult at the same time. We don't have a single word in English to describe this. We might say things like a "wise child" or a "child-like adult," but these conjunctions of opposites don't really do the paradox justice. Our language forces us to emphasize one word over the other, because one term is a noun and the other is an adjective to modify it.

The texts of Jesus' aphorism say adults enter God's kingdom "like children" or receive it "as a little child," or are born into it from above, but the aphorism's intent seems to be to force us to experience the reality of being a child and of being an adult at the same time to challenge us with a new view of human nature.

The more one tries to improve on the child/adult paradox, the more one appreciates the art and depth of Jesus' aphorism. It is probably best to just step back and admire the art in the various forms of its texts and give it a "respectful whistle" of appreciation. It is something that deserves spending more time with.

The next chapter will begin the deconstruction of the paradox by constructing concepts about children to see if we can build a bridge from what we know about them to what we don't know about being in God's kingdom. This means that, with the early theologians, we will now take a literal perspective to understand the child we are to be like to enter the kingdom.

CHAPTER 2

Considering Children as Concepts

A LITERAL VIEW OF JESUS' SAYING

The Gospels refer to entering (Matthew 18:3), receiving (Mark 10:14; Luke 18:17), and being born into (John 3:3, 7) the kingdom like children, so we need to clarify what we mean by "children" to know *what we need to be like* to be part of the kingdom. To do this we will dismantle the child/adult paradox and take only a "literal view" of "the child" that fits with the plain meaning of everyday speech. In the next chapter we will do the opposite. We will consider children in a figurative way as parables to stimulate our imagination to go beyond the ordinary meaning.

A literal *concept* about children is no more real than a menu is a meal, but we need to carefully and slowly form a general idea about them, because we were all children once.

Our intuition has been shaped by our personal experiences, which vivify but limit our view.

We need to avoid the "overconfidence" of what Daniel Kahneman called a "focusing illusion." This can be illustrated by Kahneman's study of Midwestern and Californian college students. The Midwesterners leapt to the conclusion that Californians were happier than they were, although both groups independently reported the same life satisfaction.[1] To prevent a confident leaping from illusion to conclusion, we will slow down and formalize our thinking by looking at children from four points of view: theology, history, psychology, and our own unique memories of childhood.

THEOLOGIANS AND THE GRATEFUL CHILD

Most theologians across the centuries have been ambivalent, ambiguous, and/or indifferent to children. Only a few have considered them a means of grace, which would be more in line with Jesus' saying.

I surveyed this history in *Children and the Theologians* (2009) with the hope of making this negative, unspoken, *de facto* theology of childhood more conscious.[2] Making it conscious, I thought, might clear the way to build a more constructive and graceful theology of childhood to guide the church in the future.

In this book I will concentrate on the work of a single theologian, Hans Urs von Balthasar (1905–1988), who considered children a means of grace, and placed the child's wonder at

---

1. Daniel Kahneman, *Thinking, Fast and Slow* (New York: Farrar, Straus and Giroux, 2011), 402–403.

2. Jerome W. Berryman, *Children and the Theologians: Clearing the Way for Grace* (New York: Morehouse Publishing, 2009), 8–24.

being born in the center of his enormous, theological project, which blended theology, spirituality, and beauty. He explicitly addressed the complexity of becoming-like-a-child just before he died, in a little book that we will come to in a moment.

Von Balthasar proposed that children begin to wonder when they open their eyes and see their mother's smile. The smile signifies that they are in a new home after the difficult struggle through the birth canal and that they are welcome in this new reality. Many human beings around our earth have felt this welcome by their mothers' smiles, but they have not given much thought to it in theological terms.

Von Balthasar thought that the wonder babies experience comes from "being permitted to be." He placed this experience at the center of his theology, because, as he wrote, "This condition of being permitted cannot be surpassed by any additional insight into the laws and necessities of the world."[3] Our original wonder at being alive opens us to God's undifferentiated yet creative presence focused by the mother's smile. Being alive and being welcomed are global feelings in the infant, so the resulting gratitude is a pervasive gratitude for life itself. As such, it shapes our identity, which in turn shapes how we live and do our dying.

Others have noticed the importance of gratitude for being alive as a life-shaping event. Virginia Woolf commented on this in *Moments of Being*. She wrote that "moments of being" are the times when one experiences reality itself, instead of the more ordinary protective covering, which she called "non-being."

One of Woolf's earliest "moments of being" took place when she was lying in her crib in the nursery—"half asleep, half awake"—listening to sounds beyond the window that she

---

3. Quoted in David L. Schindler, *Hans Urs von Balthasar: His Life and Work* (San Francisco: Communio, 1991), 633.

later realized were the sounds of the waves breaking—"one, two, one, two, and sending a splash of water over the beach." As she listened she also watched the light come into the room as the breeze lifted the blind. She wrote, ". . . of lying and hearing this splash and seeing this light, and feeling, it is almost impossible that I should be here; of feeling the purest ecstasy I can conceive."[4] The gratitude she felt for being alive provided the primal foundation for her life. As she said, "these moments of being of mine were scaffolding in the background; were the invisible and silent part of my life as a child."[5]

Von Balthasar discovered the starting point for his theology by watching children around him, remembering his own childhood, by his theological intuition and his enormous learning. He was also greatly aided by Adrienne von Speyr (1902–1967), a respected medical doctor in Basel, who was baptized a Roman Catholic in 1940 under his spiritual guidance when she was thirty-eight. She kept the reality of children always in front of von Balthasar and he warmly appreciated her joy, childlike qualities, and wonder—as well as her strength and courage, which were often tested by poor health and in other ways. Together they established a religious society in 1945, the secular Community of Saint John (*Johannesgemeinschaft* [*Säkularinstitut*]) for women and men. Von Balthasar wrote about the spirituality practiced there in *Our Task* (1984 German, 1994 English).[6]

---

4. Quoted in John Pridmore, *Playing with Icons: The Spirituality of Recalled Childhood*, private mss., 94. To read more fully about Virginia Woolf's foundational experience, see *Moments of Being: A Collection of Autobiographical Writing*, ed. Jeanne Schulkind (San Diego: Harcourt, A Harvest Book, second edition, 1985), 64–72. This book was edited after Woolf's death.

5. Woolf, *Moments of Being*, 73.

6. The common "task" referred to in the title is that of von Balthasar and von Speyr. Von Balthasar hoped to insure that no one would desire to separate his work from hers. The book also includes a description of the way the community was formed and its spirituality, which gives another meaning to the commonality of the task.

The Society of Jesus decided that founding a secular community of men and women was at odds with his vocation as a
Jesuit, so von Balthasar left the order with great, personal difficulty in 1950. He felt that God had called him to a new task,
which was to sanctify the world from within the secular ethos.
This move also, at least in my view, forced him to see more
clearly the importance of children for his theology.

What von Balthasar saw in children has not been the majority view in theology. St. Augustine represents the majority view,
so let's take a moment to discuss his experience with children,
which influenced his theology. The Bishop of Hippo Regius in
North Africa thought that children arrived in the world already
infected with original sin. He knew firsthand from his own
adolescence that sinfulness was a fundamental part of human
nature. He and a group of boys stole pears, merely "for the
excitement of stealing."

Augustine could not remember his own infancy to determine its sinfulness by introspection, so he watched babies to
see if they showed signs of original sin. He thought they did
and wrote, perhaps with irony, "The feebleness of infant limbs
is innocent, not the infant's mind."[7] In other words, he thought
babies and children may look innocent, but in reality the evidence of their self-love and diseased wills, as when they are
hungrily feeding at the breast without concern for others, show
that they are born sinful. Today we might call such infant
behavior an instinct, which is necessary for survival, but some
1,500 years ago Augustine saw something else.

Augustine also learned about children as a father and par-
ticipant in a marriage of some thirteen years. This was a legal

7. Augustine, *Confessions*, trans. Henry Chadwick (Oxford, UK: Oxford University
Press: World's Classics edition, 1992), 9. His description of watching infants at the breast
is also on page 9. The description of stealing pears "for the excitement of stealing" is at
page 29.

marriage, but it was not fully and strictly connected to the laws of Roman citizenship and inheritance. Like many in the Roman Empire, he opted for a second-class marriage, which had the official sanction of the church, until he was ready to commit to the stringency of the more formal one.[8] Augustine never mentioned his wife's name in all his voluminous writing, but the child they had together was called Adeodatus (A Gift from God). He did not have much if anything to say about the details of his own son's sinfulness except that he was born out of Augustine's sin.

Bishop Ambrose baptized Adeodatus and his father at the cathedral in Milan during the Easter Vigil in 387. Augustine later praised his sixteen-year-old son for his part in the dialogue *The Teacher*, which Augustine said they wrote together about 389, not long after the two of them returned to North Africa. Adeodatus' mother had been sent back to Africa earlier when Augustine decided to marry a young, Roman heiress, but the marriage never took place. Sadly, Adeodatus died in Africa at an age only a little older than his father had been when he and his friends had stolen pears a generation before.

We will return to Augustine many times as this book unfolds, but for now we will just note one more thing. It was the voice of *a child*, chanting over and over again "Pick up and read,"[9] that was the means of grace for his conversion. Upon hearing the child's chanting, he opened "the book of the apostle" and read from Romans 13:13–14, which was the catalyst for his conversion to Christianity.

---

8. "Concubinage" was a traditional feature of Roman life, and the Catholic Church recognized it, provided the couple remained faithful to one another." This second-class marriage with a concubine (not a prostitute) was for convenience until one was established in life and ready to take on the responsibilities of a Roman citizen. Peter Brown, *Augustine of Hippo* (Berkeley, CA: University of California Press, 1967), 62.

9. Augustine, *Confessions*, 152.

This short digression highlights the difference between von Balthasar's view of children and Augustine's. This contrast shows how radical it was for von Balthasar to write that the mother's smile shows the infant "that it is contained, affirmed, and loved in a relationship which is incomprehensively encompassing, already actual, sheltering, and nourishing." As an "object of love," the child feels allowed to be and begins to play.

The experience of "being permitted" precedes questions about rights and duties, so children's gratitude for being is the deep root for adult ethical consciousness. "Everything, without exception, which is to follow later and will inevitably be added to this experience must remain an unfolding of it."[10] We will return to this idea in chapter 5 when we discuss Thomas Traherne, who placed the gratitude of the child at the center of his theory of ethics for adults.

When von Balthasar died at the age of eighty-three, the manuscript for a little book was found on his desk. He had planned to give it to friends as a Christmas present. In English it is called *Unless You Become Like This Child*, and with it von Balthasar added another dimension to Jesus' call for us to become like a child. We also need to become like *this child*, the Christ child, to dwell in God's kingdom.

We know almost nothing about Jesus' early years, despite many attempts over the centuries by historians, artists, novelists, and poets to reconstruct them. A bridge between the centuries, however, exists. It is play. Von Balthasar wrote that Jesus and all children play naturally like Sophia did. She (Holy Wisdom) has played in God's presence since the beginning of time and was personified in Proverbs (8:22–31).

---

10. Hans Urs von Balthasar, *The Glory of the Lord: A Theological Aesthetics, V: The Realm of Metaphysics in the Modern Age* (San Francisco: Ignatius Press, 1991), 616.

Von Balthasar thought that the playful blend of Sofia, the Christ Child, and all children, regardless of time or place, pleases God and "exactly fulfills his command."[11] God's Child embodied God's *command* to play *freely*, which defines our nature and avoids the either-or thinking (predestination versus free will) about grace that has sometimes dominated theology.

Von Balthasar's view of grace, much like that of St. Thomas in his *Summa Theologiae*,[12] was that we are *determined* by God to choose freely, as creators in God's image, so the grace of God's love can be accepted (instead of overwhelming us) and nourish us creatively all through our lives and in our deaths. We will return to the theme of play when we discuss the psychological view of children later in this chapter, and in chapter 4 when we talk about how the creative process plays pervasively in God's creation.

In summary, then, von Balthasar is a strong representative of the minority view in Christian theology concerning the nature of children. He stressed that their nature is one of gratitude for being permitted to be. It is from this source that our ethics emerges and our life and death is framed. The mother's smile and our tendency to play are the accent notes in his theology of childhood. These themes will continue to appear in this book, but it is now time to turn to the historians of childhood, whose method is much different from that of theology.

---

11. Hans Urs von Balthasar, *Unless You Become Like This Child* (San Francisco: Communio, 1991), 35–36.

12. Denys Turner, *Thomas Aquinas: A Portrait* (New Haven, CT: Yale University Press, 2013), 154.

HISTORIANS AND THE RELATIONAL CHILD

We began to discuss the difference between theologians and historians in the last chapter with the story about Ritschl and his son-in-law. We also noted how Albert Schweitzer integrated both points of view within his own life. Just a few more words of introduction are needed about the difference between the methods of theologians and historians.

Theology makes meaning by consulting scripture and tradition, the use of reason, and by prayer and experience, especially the experience of God's presence. As you can see, much of this method involves past events which shape present awareness. Events happened—such as Christmas, Easter, and Pentecost for Christians—that are still participated in liturgically and studied to guide life in the present and to plan for the future. The Christians' past in the first century was shaped by an older past—the Torah, wisdom, poetry, and liturgical practice of the Hebrew People, which goes all the way back to the beginning, as told in Genesis.

There is a great deal of respect for the past in theology. Tradition is one of its major sources of knowledge, which sometimes involves a longing for the "purity" of the church in its earliest form. We all yearn for a "golden age" when things were better or even perfect, but when the respect for the past drifts into nostalgia, it can alter our historical memory and distort our view of the present and the future.

In 2004 Stephen Mintz wrote in *Huck's Raft: A History of American Childhood* that "nostalgia for the past offers no solutions to the problems of the present."[13] He hoped that his study of childhood would help us understand children today,

---

13. Stephen Mintz, *Huck's Raft: A History of American Childhood*, (Cambridge, MA: Harvard University Press, 2004), 382.

but to do so it had to be accurate. Without the knowledge of what really happened, we are doomed to repeat the tragedies of history. Even if history never repeats itself exactly, its perspective always helps us understand the present and plan for the future.

Those who study history avoid nostalgia and other distortions of the past by looking for artifacts and written sources to anchor their interpretations. The history of childhoods past involve the analysis of such things as paintings, handbooks on childrearing, the journals of parents and children, laws concerning children, children's toys, the privacy implied by the structure of dwellings, and finding household objects related to children such as walkers and potties for toddlers and a breast-shaped, clay bottle for feeding infants, discovered in a seventh century grave in England.

Historians have been ingenious, working within their method to illuminate the past. For example, there were no death rates for children compiled in England during the Middle Ages. If we assume survival was no better than a few centuries later, we can say that about one in four babies died during their first year. About half of all children died before reaching the age of ten. Statistics like this are important, but they don't give us "a feel" for these deaths. Barbara Hanawalt changed that when she used coroners' records from four parts of England to study accidental death.

The accident most children died from during their first year was from burning up in their cribs, placed next to the open fire to keep them warm while their parents were away. Children about two years of age were more mobile—crawling, toddling, and walking, so they died mostly from falling into wells, drowning in ponds, or scalding themselves with boiling water. From four to seven years, most deaths came from accidents at play, like getting a ball from a gutter along the edge of a high roof. After seven years of age, the boys were mostly injured at work in the fields and in other apprenticeships while the girls were injured at home or in other homes where they worked.[14]

Having a feel for the past helps us gain perspective on our lives today by contrast. It is astonishing that we can monitor our infants in their cribs electronically and we have central heating and plumbing so children do not burn up in their cribs or fall down wells. In developed countries we are not as likely as medieval parents to be concerned about the threat to our children from wild animals, unexplained sickness, freezing to death, starvation, and thirst, but we are concerned about protecting children from human predators and children being absorbed into the two-dimensional electronic world, which often deflects relationships with real people and personal involvement in the natural world.

We also have much in common with parents in the past. We share grief at the loss of our little ones, and we too worry about teething, illness, accidents, and children growing up to be responsible, mature adults. Life in the family has changed in some ways since the Middle Ages, and in other ways it has not.

Interest in medieval children began to grow when Philippe Ariès (1914–1984) published *L'Enfant et la vie familiale sous l'Ancien Regime* in 1960. It was published in English in 1962 as *Centuries of Childhood* and was more widely read and

---

14. Referenced in Hugh Cunningham, *Children and Childhood in Western Society Since 1500* (London: Longman, 1995), 38–39.

Hanawalt wrote, "The more we wish to penetrate into the lives of ordinary people, the more complex our use of sources becomes. With this increasing complexity, the challenge of writing and of holding the attention of nonspecialists becomes even greater." To solve this problem she began to use "composite characters," which she discussed in the "Preface" to her *Growing Up in Medieval London: The Experience of Childhood in History* (Oxford, UK: Oxford University Press, 1993), viii–ix.

authoritative in the English-speaking world than in France. Ariès argued that children were freer and happier in medieval times than today because they were more integrated into the family. There was no *idea of childhood* to set them apart.

Children were not considered fully human during the baby-toddler stage, because they lacked speech, did not have full control over their movement, and their social awareness was lacking. As they grew they entered a proto-adult stage when they were considered to be like adults, only smaller and less competent, so their responsibilities were assigned accordingly. David Lancy, an anthropologist who has studied children and their families worldwide, commented, "This characterization is probably not far off the mark for peasant society throughout much of civilization."[15]

Ariès claimed that by the seventeenth century adults began to worry about "civilizing" children, which objectified them and made them less part of their families. The growing concept of childhood continued to be elaborated in the centuries that followed, so children were further pushed out of their families into schools and other institutions outside of the family. In our time, for example, we have lawyers and doctors who specialize in the problems of children. In the Middle Ages such specialization was unheard of except for wet nurses, who have now disappeared. Ariès' view of children in the Middle Ages shocked people. The field quickly expanded, largely to prove him wrong.[16]

---

15. David F. Lancy, *The Anthropology of Childhood: Cherubs, Chattel, Changelings*, second edition (Cambridge: Cambridge University Press, 2015), 5.

16. Ariès did not just help originate the history of childhood. His book *Western Attitudes Toward Death* (1974) paved the way for this field of history as well. In addition he continued to work on the history of childhood. Please note: Philippe Aries and Georges Duby, eds., *A History of Private Life*, 5 volumes (Cambridge, MA: Harvard University Press, 1992–1994).

Lloyd de Mause (1931) was one of the earliest voices to contradict Ariès. He edited and contributed to *The History of Childhood* published in 1974. His study included ancient times to the present in the West and concluded that children have grown happier during modern times.

De Mause used a controversial method he called "psycho-history" to show how the treatment of children has moved through six "psychogenic modes" from infanticide, to abandonment, to ambivalence, to intrusive, to socializing, and finally to helping. He wrote that the "history of childhood is a nightmare from which we have only recently begun to awaken," and he contrasted his view explicitly with that of Ariès. Families have integrated their children more today than in centuries past, he argued, and children have become happier.

The movement of history is seldom as straightforward as Ariès' and de Mause's contrasting views. John Sommerville demonstrated that there has been continuous evidence of adults being aware of children since the Egyptians, but he wrote in *The Rise and Fall of Childhood* (1982) that the glorification of children rose and fell over the centuries. During the nineteenth century in England, this idealism rose to unprecedented heights, but at the same time children were brutally exploited in the mills and mines.

William Beechey, a successful painter to the aristocracy and royalty, painted a large painting (180–150 cm) of Sir Francis Ford's two children around 1793. The Ford children were well scrubbed and splendidly dressed in elaborate, satin finery, fashionable hats, and elegant shoes. The painting shows them giving an older, stooped, barefoot, dirty beggar boy a coin. He probably had no family except for the children in the streets.

The painting was intended to promote pity, sympathy, and kindness for impoverished children, and to encourage and laud the generosity of the aristocracy. It looks like the Ford children were happy and pleased with themselves, but the sickly beggar boy is harder to read. He is deferential but confused at confronting such self-assured, pampered children. He seems to lack gratitude and is sad but stunned at these creatures from another world. This was an age when beggars were usually painted as pathetic, so this boy may be the most complex and interesting part of the painting by a prosperous but second-rank portrait painter, whose contemporaries were Gainsborough and Joshua Reynolds.

Beechey's painting needs to be hung alongside an enlarged print from the 1842 Royal Commission on Children Employed in Mines and Manufactories to contrast the worlds of children during this period. The Mines and Manufactories print shows children in the county of Lancashire in the industrial northwest of England. One boy crawls in front, pulling a coal cart, with two boys pushing it from behind. They covered four to six miles a day on "roads," which were actually tunnels only about twenty inches high. In 1851 there were 24,247 children under the age of fifteen working in coal mines under these conditions in England and Wales.[17]

A modern version of the two worlds of childhood would not be a painting of aristocratic children giving a pittance to a beggar. It would be a photograph of a malnourished slave child in Cote d'Ivoire harvesting "the cocoa beans that will be processed into the chocolates consumed by obese children in the West."[18]

Concepts of childhood seep into children's consciousness from the culture. Hugh Cunningham illustrated this by quoting from eleven-year-old Zlata's diary during the siege of

---

17. Hugh Cunningham, *The Invention of Childhood* (London: BBC Books, 2006), opposite 208.

18. Lancy, *The Anthropology of Childhood*, 378.

Sarajevo. He wrote, "Zlata had a clear sense of the ingredients of a childhood: innocence, school, fun, games, friends, nature, sweets. Deprived of them, she wrote, she and her friends 'can't be children.'" In her mind she was "not simply someone aged between, say, birth and fourteen; a child could be a real child only if he or she had a 'childhood.'"[19]

The British historian R. H. Tawney (1880–1962) asked an important question for any society in any age when he wrote famously in *Religion and the Rise of Capitalism* that "the treatment of childhood" shows most clearly "the true character of a social philosophy" held by any society. Many governments in the world today lack interest, resources, and public support to be concerned about children.

Tawney's political view of the need to care for children in the West, however, does illustrate how vast the network is that influences how the family sustains its children. This wider network in England included advice about child rearing, the church's social programs to support children and families, the work of secular charities, and the influence of state-run programs to provide such things as schooling, mental health, medical care, and child protective services.

Some people in the nineteenth century were shocked that poor children did not have a childhood, in terms of the Ford children. They campaigned for poor, working (and thieving) children "to have a childhood." In the twenty-first century the old ideal of childhood is disappearing, but children are still cared about and cared for.

Somerville argued that historians notice something "just as it is about to disappear . . . to preserve it in our memory."[20] This

---

19. Cunningham, *Centuries of Childhood*, 1.

20. John Sommerville, *The Rise and Fall of Childhood* (Beverly Hills, CA: Sage Publications, 1982), 7.

partially accounts for our interest in the history of childhood. Somerville's *The Rise and Fall of Childhood* was published in 1982, the same year Neil Postman first published *The Disappearance of Childhood*. Postman also observed that histories are produced when an event is waning and unlikely to reoccur. He wrote, "Historians usually come not to praise but to bury."[21]

During the decade after Somerville and Postman published their books, Richard Louv also worried about the disappearance of the childhood he had known. He spent three years interviewing children and parents about this and concluded that childhood, as he had experienced it, was evaporating. Instead of grieving, he looked ahead in *Childhood's Future* (1991) and talked about "weaving a new web" so that children could be engaged in "positive adult contact and a sense of connection to the wider human community." This sounds something like the ideal of what Ariès thought the experience of children was like during the Middle Ages. Louv went on to argue that children "need positive independence and solitude (as opposed to ongoing isolation) and a sense of wonder"[22] to fashion a new and constructive kind of childhood. He has continued to work to reconnect families, children, and nature with such books as *Last Child in the Woods: Saving Our Children from Nature Deficit Disorder* (2008).

Postman and Louv both argued for involving children in the re-weaving of new and more beneficial relationships between children and adults and with nature. What they may not have realized is that, in other parts of the world, children have already begun to fashion a future out of necessity that we would hardly recognize as a "childhood."

---

21. Neil Postman, *The Disappearance of Childhood* (New York: Vintage Books, 1994), 5.

22. Richard Louv, *Childhood's Future* (New York: Doubleday, 1991), 173.

For example in Tanzania the major cities are flooded with some 300,000 street children. The study of "street kids" is in its infancy, but it is clear that the slang, ways of dressing, learning by observing, and living in non-biological "families" of children show the outlines of the new culture they are fashioning, even if it sounds a bit like the London that Dickens evoked in his novels.

The other non-biological "family" option for many children around the world is to become soldiers. They are recruited/ abducted and join roving bands as a matter of survival. These victims become aggressors. In Sierra Leone children were responsible for thousands of murders, mutilations, and rapes, and for torture, forced labor, and sexual slavery.[23] When they are captured they pose a tragic problem. How should they be treated? Are they children or adults? Victims or aggressors?

About the same time that Somerville and Postman published their books, Linda Pollack published *Forgotten Children*. She found historical continuity in the way parents loved, grieved, worried about, and reared their children from 1500–1900, despite the great changes in society, such as the Industrial Revolution in England and the U.S. Pollack's finding adds a fourth alternative to Ariès' downward trend of positive awareness of children and their integration in their families, the upward trend found by de Mauss, and Somerville's up and down trends. It is worth taking a moment to expand on Pollack's study.

She began her study with the big picture, which involved sociobiology, primate studies, and anthropology. The pressures of evolution have pushed most human parents toward various forms of "attachment," a deep and enduring bond with their children. This involves such actions as protection, affection, play, and training.

---

23. Lancy, *The Anthropology of Childhood*, 386.

To stay close to the experience of actual families, Pollock consulted 416 private and public diaries of adults and children as well as autobiographies. She found that "there have been very few changes in parental care and child life in the home from the sixteenth through the nineteenth century despite social changes and technological improvements."[24] Strategies for parenting changed, but parents continued to worry about their family's future, to grieve over their children's illness or death, and only occasionally used brutality in punishment.

Not all historians are in agreement about the validity of Pollack's sources, even though they may agree with her conclusion. Hugh Cunningham cautioned that children's diaries can tell "us more about the genre of diary writing and the desires and expectations of adult readers than about the experience of being a child."[25] An inner editing by children and parents about what they ought to write takes place and there is an outer editing by professional editors for publication, who would like to sell books to the public. The use of texts also limits the study to those who can read and write, which in the years from 1500–1900 usually meant the upper classes. We might also wonder what parents actually said to their children, since writing is so different from speaking. Alas, we will never know.

Perhaps, the greatest example of continuity in the care of children comes from Sommerville. He quoted from a letter written by a father to his son. The father wrote, "Go to school. Stand before your teacher, recite your assignment, open your schoolbag, write your tablet, let the teacher's assistant write your new lesson for you. . . . Don't stand about in the public

24. Linda A. Pollock, *Forgotten Children: Parent-Child Relations from 1500–1900* (Cambridge: Cambridge University Press, 1983), 268.

25. Cunningham, *Children and Childhood in Western Society Since 1500*, 2.

square."[26] This "letter" was pressed into clay about 1800 BCE and found in the Mesopotamian Valley. The son was learning to be a scribe, but the father's concerns sound contemporary, even after some 3,817 years.

In summary, then, we can say that there is no such thing as "a child." This is because no child stands alone, even among the street children who seek out other children to parent them and teach them the ways of their street culture. Children need to be part of a life-giving and intimate network that bonds them with their parents and other caregivers or they will likely perish or fail to thrive. This network that influences children and their parents extends in the West to the highest levels of government and draws on a concept of childhood, created by this vast network, which defines childhood and shapes the experience of living children.

One of the ways that children maintain the networks of relationships that sustain them is through play, which anthropologist David Lancy called "a truly universal trait of childhood."[27] This is the one thing that children can do for themselves without the sanction of culture or the blessing of parents. A few theologians and many historians have become interested in play, but the psychologists are the ones who have understood that play is a major diagnostic and health-giving experience. We turn to their views now.

PSYCHOLOGISTS AND THE PLAYFUL CHILD

Historians cannot tell us much directly about the inner worlds of infants and young children because their method is limited to texts and artifacts. To gain better access to children's inner experience, we need to consult the child psychologists.

---

26. Sommerville, *The Rise and Fall of Childhood*, 21–22.
27. Lancy, *The Anthropology of Childhood*, 19.

The field of child psychology began with the baby biographers in the nineteenth century, among them Charles Darwin. The field expanded greatly during the twentieth century, but this expansion moved in all directions without a comprehensive, overarching theory. William Kessen (1925–1999) emphasized this diversity when he gave his presidential address to the American Psychological Association's Division of Developmental Psychology in 1978 and expanded on this theme in 1981 at the Fourth Houston Symposium when he observed that "the child is essentially and eternally a cultural invention."[28]

Kessen argued that the reason there is no overarching theory for child psychology is because the culture has not supported it. Kessen summed up the variety of theories used by child psychologists in a down-to-earth way. He said that Charles Darwin observed his son Doddy and found emotions. James Mark Baldwin observed his daughter Polly and found thoughts. Sigmund Freud observed Ann and found wish fulfillment, while John Watson observed Billy and found unconditioned responses. When Jean Piaget observed Jacqueline, he found adaptive assimilation, but when B. F. Skinner observed Debra, he saw a baby in a box of stimulus and response. Kessen added wryly that theories about children are not inhibited if the scholar does not have children. John Locke was a bachelor and Jean-Jacques Rousseau sent his five children to the Paris foundling home as soon as they were born.[29]

Infants and toddlers absorb this confusion about their nature nonverbally, mostly from their parents, but they deal with it like they deal with learning about balance as they begin

---

28. Kessen also expressed these views in "The American Child and Other Cultural Inventions," *American Psychologist*, 1979, 34 (10), 815–820.

29. Frank S. Kessel and Alexander W. Siegel, eds., *The Child and Other Cultural Inventions* (New York: Praeger Publishers, 1983), 28.

to walk. They play through it. In fact, it is play that enables us to work through our developmental crises during the whole life span.

Play's contribution to human development begins when children learn to trust the "world" (mostly the mother) by poking, nuzzling, and playing with it. They also make strides as toddlers to become independent through play. Erik Erikson called the preschool years from about three to five years of age "the play age," because he thought play was especially important at that time. It helps children develop skills, fantasy, cooperation, and how to lead as well as follow. They also work through the fundamental crisis for this period, which he identified as initiative versus guilt. Passing through this gate successfully enables children to act with purpose.

Erikson identified the time spent in school from about five-to-twelve years of age as the crisis of industry versus inferiority. This results in competence when successfully resolved. The point is that play helps healthy development because you can try out different ways of dealing with a psychosocial crisis by reframing it in a noncritical way. Reframing a crisis in the play frame gives it an as-if quality, which shifts a situation full of judgment and conflicting emotions to one that is open, full of energy, and fun.

Adolescents, who take themselves very seriously as they seek a new and more adequate sense of self, are greatly in need of playfulness to help resolve their adolescent identity crisis. Play in this situation helps develop a sense of what Erikson called "fidelity," which is the ability to commit one's self to others even when there are differences.

Play is also important as adults mature through early (intimacy vs. isolation), middle (generativity vs. stagnation), and late adulthood (ego integrity vs. despair). The danger for older adults is that their self-absorption with their losses—social, personal, and physical—causes an inability to play, which is accompanied by the loss of one's sense of humor. This inhibits gaining perspective on oneself. Perspective is needed to successfully resolve the integrity versus despair crisis, so one can become an elder rather than just elderly. Play gives seasoned elders the ability to see life and death from many perspectives with a knowing smile.

Erik Erikson died in 1994 at the age of ninety-one, and his wife Joan died in 1997 at the age of ninety-four. As the Eriksons lived through their eighties, they realized how unique this time of life was. Joan, who was a strong advocate of play and a sense of humor, pioneered most of the writing about the ninth stage in *The Life Cycle Completed: Extended Version* (1997). She drew on her experience as a ninety-three-year-old elder to describe how the eight crises during former decades, such as trust vs. mistrust, reverse in priority in the ninth stage. Elders begin to mistrust their own capabilities because their body can no longer be trusted. The trust reversal becomes key to the final stage, and the resolution of mistrust vs. trust brings with it a sense of blessing. Play, as you can see, is a powerful theme that runs all through optimum human development to the end.

Child psychologists have long understood this. They have seen children reveal themselves through play, and they understand how play helps them heal when they are hurt or confused. Even a schedule of reinforcement, used by a behaviorist, or medication administered by a psychiatrist, works better if applied and supported in a playful way.

Play bridges the worlds of adults and children despite differences in size, experience, emotional maturity, and cognitive development. It can also bridge the centuries, since humans and other mammals have played for millennia. This makes one wonder if Jesus, as a child and an adult, played with the children he met.

We do know that the disciples did not play. They were too self-absorbed to play with Jesus' odd ideas about the kingdom and they even tried to send the children away rather than learn from them. All they could do, at least at first, was ask serious, culture-bound questions about who was going to be most important in the kingdom Jesus was talking about. They were attracted to, as well as disgusted by, the threat of Roman power and the authority of the religious establishment in Jerusalem. Jesus invited them to play their way into the kingdom, like children, and showed them how, but they did not understand this. Eventually they did learn, but this shows how difficult understanding what Jesus was saying is for adults, even when Jesus is your personal mentor!

Despite the power of play, there is something ambiguous about it. At first this seems like a deficiency, but it is really the root of its power. The ambiguity comes from the fact that there is no particular *activity* that can be isolated as playful. We can turn anything we do into play, so work can become play, but play can't be work and still be play.

Play's ambiguity was confronted directly by Brian Sutton-Smith (1924–2015) in 1997 after about five decades of experience and study that began in Wellington, New Zealand, as a young man. As he said, "We all play occasionally, and we all know what playing feels like. But when it comes to making theoretical statements about what play is, we fall into silliness." Nevertheless, he began to theorize about play in 1942 and continued for the rest of his life, trying to get it right.

Sutton-Smith thought he finally got his theory right in 1997 with his book *The Ambiguity of Play*, which was published when he was in his early seventies. He suggested we use seven identifiable ways or "rhetorics" to understand play. This variety of viewpoints arises out of and explains play's ambiguity. Four of his rhetorics were ancient views—playing for power as in athletic contests, playing with fate as in gambling, playing as ritual that symbolically informs community identity as in religion, and playing as the utter frivolity of the "idle or the foolish." Three modern theories of play, developed after about 1800, saw it as integral to human development, as self-engaged such as in high-risk sports, and as improvisation with the imagination in many areas of life from chemistry, to stand-up comedy, to child rearing.

At the beginning of *The Ambiguity of Play*, Sutton-Smith promised a more unified theory, despite play's seven rhetorics. His conclusion was that play is "adaptive variability."[30] It produces the variability that reopens evolution's possibilities when we get stuck. Evolution's selection for survival requires the creation of alternatives to select from. Play is the human reenactment of this larger selection process in the individual lives of our species. It is always specific to what is being played, but is also always broader in this evolutionary sense to find the best path forward. We will return to these ideas in chapter 4 when we talk about the pervasiveness of the creative process in the world and in chapter 5 when we talk about steering between chaos and rigidity as maturity beyond the norm.

Despite Sutton-Smith's defining theory about play, we need a more practical description so we can know play when we encounter it in others and ourselves. Catherine Garvey's description is as accurate as it is succinct. Play is pleasurable, voluntary, done for itself, alters our ordinary sense of

---

30. Brian Sutton-Smith, *The Ambiguity of Play* (Cambridge, MA: Harvard University Press, 1997), 221.

time, is absorbing, and has connections to creativity, learning languages, learning social roles, and solving problems.[31] We need to add one more factor to Garvey's list. Play is signaled nonverbally.

Sometimes people try to deceive potential "playmates" with talk about play, so the invitation is not honest. It is a deceitful device to take advantage of people who might let down their guard and become vulnerable if they think they are going to play. When people betray the trust that is required for play, they become pseudo-players who might talk a good game but are not able to play or they do not intend to play. The only way to tell if play is genuine is to assess the initial "play-face" and then continue to monitor all aspects of nonverbal communication to see if the play state continues.

Children quickly learn by intuition to tell who knows how to play and who doesn't, because this is critical to their enjoyment of life, health, and development. Sometimes children don't want to go to a friend's house because they and their family don't know how to play, but the child doesn't know how to put that into words. They just know that such people aren't any fun, so they fuss and try to avoid getting taken there.

It is disappointing to realize that play can be faked for ulterior motives, but it is more disappointing to understand that the creative aspect of play can be used for destructive purposes. I would like to mention four ways this takes place.

First, play and creativity can be misused in anti-social ways. Those involved in theft, deception, and intimidation, even for trivial things, enjoy the excitement and creativity associated with play. Mihaly Csikszentmihalyi called attention to this

---

31. Catherine Garvey, *Play: The Developing Child*, second edition (Cambridge, MA: Harvard University Press, 1990), 5.

misuse in a collection of essays by various authors called *Optimal Experience* (1988). One of the essays by Ikuya Sato specifically described the pleasant flow of creativity in Japanese motorcycle gangs.

Play also becomes destructive by addiction. Stuart Brown described and warned about the dangers of "play addicts" in his book *Play* (2009).[32] When children become addicted to screen games, such as "playing" computer games, the activity is no longer play, even if we use the word "play" to describe it. This is because it is no longer voluntary. It is a compulsion.

A third way play becomes destructive is when those who engage in games must win at any cost, even if they have to break the rules and destroy the spirit of the game to do so. This turns play into work for them and for those trying to play with them. Play is meant to be in the service of human development, not its destruction.

Finally, people can be explicitly paid to play games to entertain others, as in professional sports. We often hear professional athletes describe the pain they felt when they first truly realized that the game they loved to play was really a business. Even in professional sports, however, we find moments when the game is clearly played for the love of it and not just for the financial payoff. The *business* of games can be transcended so that the game is, once again, played for itself and the pleasure of playing.

In summary, play expresses the image of the Creator we carry within us. It takes a great deal of playfulness and creativity to imagine and live in the alternative reality Jesus spoke of in his aphorism. It is a kingdom of seeds, weeds, treasures, pearls, fish, and leaven that invites us to open our minds to enter, receive, and/or be born into maturity beyond the norm.

---

32. Stuart Brown, *Play: How It Shapes the Brain, Opens the Imagination, and Invigorates the Soul* (New York: Penguin, 2009), 183–189.

ADULTS AND THE REMEMBERED CHILD

We have discussed the wondrous experience of being permitted to be and the gratitude that flows from it. We have examined how children are necessarily relational creatures as infants and throughout their lives. Play was discussed as fundamental to human development, especially the health and development of children. This brings us to our unique, personal memories of childhood. They ground the above generalizations and bring our uniqueness into the foreground. The way to know the "remembered child" is to tell stories from our past and to reflect on them. We will begin with an example from my life, which I hope will encourage you to stop for a moment in your reading to reflect on your own childhood before proceeding.

The broken bird's egg was all that mattered. I knelt down in the green grass beside its sky-blue pieces. One end was smooth and round and lovely. The other was jagged, sharp, and terrifying. Inside the rounded part some yellow yoke glowed with life. It was moist and fresh, mixed with some white matter.

I can still hear my mother's voice calling in the distance, but my skin tingled with the discovery, and I did not respond. No intrusion, explanation, or affirmation was welcome. I knew the egg had fallen from the nest's tangled circle of twigs above, but all that mattered was the life and death in the grass.

The little bird had died before it was born, and I was sad, because I was still alive. It wasn't fair, but I also knew that far, far away at the edge of everything, death waited for me, too. I could not change that. There was no attempt to work this out consciously. I just let it be. I didn't tell anyone about this discovery until now. I wanted to be *in* it, not talk *about* it. Talk would break its living unity into pieces, like the shell.

I had experienced a unified kind of knowing.[33] Many have such experiences, especially during childhood. Their significance remains even if the details fade. The gratitude Virginia Woolf felt was joined to the sound of the waves and the shifting light. It takes time, patience, and a gentle openness to recover such memories, and it takes a love of language to express them in all their richness.

The difficulty of remembering significant childhood moments deserves our respect. We may not want to remember them because they are tragically painful or unbearably beautiful. Some memories fade because life rushes on, but another difficulty is that our memories reconstruct rather than reproduce. For example, psychiatrist Daniel Offer asked a group of high school students questions about their lives. Thirty-four years later he asked them the same questions. Only twenty-five percent of the grown men remembered that religion had been important to them as adolescents. During high school seventy percent of them reported that religion was important.[34]

We might call another difficulty the "philosophical block." It is caused by a focus on the adult knower, as emphasized by Rene Descartes in the seventeenth century, rather than on what is being absorbed, like Martin Heidegger emphasized in the early twentieth century, remembering back to his version

---

33. Unitive or mystical knowing takes place in the unconscious, which allows the meaning and the experience to remain a single unit. If the unity becomes consciousness in language, it retains a sense of surplus meaning no matter what is said. Said or not said, the unity continues to function unconsciously as a whole. This is a healthy kind of knowing. It is not pathology. Neither is it inferior cognition, nor a regression, not even in the service of the ego. It is a powerful, positive, and unique kind of knowing. See Dan Merkur, *Mystical Moments and Unitive Thinking* (Albany, NY: State University of New York Press, 1999), 55–59.

34. Ben Yagoda, *Memoir: A History* (New York: Riverhead Books, 2009), 103–104.

of Greek philosophy. Children absorb what emanates from beyond them naturally, because they have not yet developed the ability to block this. Heidegger had trouble expressing this idea, as we all do. (Take this paragraph for example.)[35]

Heidegger was careful to never use Christian terminology, at least after 1927,[36] but he was fascinated by the work of Johann Scheffler (1624–1677),[37] whose *The Cherubinic Wanderer* was published in 1657. It included several poems about roses being open to sunlight, like the soul is open to God's grace. The rose blooms without paying attention to itself or asking anyone to pay attention to it.[38] Heidegger advocated for adults to become the "rose without why," which is something children do naturally.

It is, of course, possible for some adults to absorb the world around them like children. Paul Cezanne (1839–1906) painted the presence of Mont Sainte-Victoire more than sixty times in

---

35. Heidegger called the radiating presence from beyond we seek to know a "showing forth," "a shinning forth," "*physis*," "*aletheia*," "*logos*," "*erignis*," "*Es gibt*," "letting," "opening," a "manifestation," an "unfolding," and a "gleaming stream," but he was never satisfied. Richard Capobianco, *Heidegger's Way of Being* (Toronto: University of Toronto Press, 2014), 92–94.

36. Thomas Sheehan, "Heidegger and Christianity" in *The Cambridge Dictionary of Christianity*, ed. Daniel Patte (Cambridge: Cambridge University Press, 2010). Heidegger was raised a Roman Catholic and studied briefly for the Catholic priesthood (1909–1911); he unsuccessfully sought a Catholic chair of philosophy in 1915. Sheehan observed, "His lecture 'Phenomenology and Theology' (1927) mandated a strict separation between faith and philosophy and between God and being—a Lutheran position that Heidegger maintained throughout his career."

37. Scheffler was raised a Lutheran and earned a medical degree from the University of Padua, but he wrote under the name Angelus Silesius after converting to Roman Catholicism in 1653. He became a Franciscan friar and priest in 1661. In 1671 he entered a Jesuit house where he remained to his death.

38. *Die Ros ist ohn warum; sie bluhet weil sie bluhet, Sie acht nicht ihrer selbst, fragt nich, ob man sie siehet.*

The rose is without "why"; it blooms simply because it blooms. It pays no attention to itself, nor does it ask whether anyone sees it.

many styles.[39] Any one of these paintings exudes a surplus of visual awareness that overflows what might be said about it. Cezanne was at peace with this. He merely returned to Mont Sainte-Victoire and painted it over and over again.

Children are like Cezanne, or Cezanne was like children. Richard N. Coe studied this kind of knowing in children. He read some 600 autobiographies of childhood in many languages. He called this kind of literature "Childhoods" and used it to construct a vision of childhood cognition, which involves unified, participatory knowing as an important characteristic.

Coe wrote that children's knowing cannot be "conveyed by the utilitarian logic of the responsible adult," because childhood "constitutes an alternative dimension" in which the wholeness of an "inner, symbolic truth" has been discovered. The world speaks to the child and the child answers, not the other way around. The difficulty of putting this knowing into words is what makes writing authentic Childhoods so difficult. As we have already said, one needs the patience to tease out the significant memories but also a love of words to express what is intimated in the remembered experience.[40]

We often underestimate the unitive knowing of children. This is because they are often attracted to what is tiny, but remain silent about the vastness they sense there. Adults sometimes "forget" such experiences "when the grass was taller," so they don't expect to see the cosmic in the small, like William Blake did when he wrote about seeing "a World in a Grain of Sand" and "a Heaven in a Wild Flower." When this ability *to see in wholes* is coupled with the language and art to express it,

---

39. Richard Capobianco used the Cezanne example in *Heidegger's Way of Being*, 42.

40. Richard N. Coe, *When the Grass Was Taller: Autobiography and the Experience of Childhood* (New Haven CT: Yale University Press, 1984), 2.

then adults can be reminded of what they used to know, how they knew it, and what it meant to them.

When we listen to children trying to say things like Blake did, we seldom have the calm curiosity and supportive patience to listen to them all the way through as they struggle to articulate their experience. We often consider their "poetry" to be no more than a vocabulary deficiency or cognitive failure. This is why children often give up and choose not to speak theologically. They fear fracturing the unity of the meaning they have experienced, and they fear its desecration by the passive dismissal or active ridicule of adults. Children prefer *being*, like the rose without why, to talking, so we often miss their moments of significance and "forget" our own. When you and I miss these moments of significance in the children around us and in our own childhoods, we miss the opportunity to hold infinity in our hands and experience eternity in an hour.[41]

---

41. "Auguries of Innocence" was written about 1803 by William Blake (1757–1827) and was found in a notebook, now called "The Pickering Manuscript." It was published in 1863 after his death and begins with:

To see a World in a Grain of Sand
And a Heaven in a Wild Flower
Hold Infinity in the palm of your hand
And Eternity in an hour.

In 1863 Alfred, Lord Tennyson wrote "Flower in the crannied wall" at Waggoners Wells near the wishing well:

Flower in the crannied wall,
I pluck you out of the crannies,
I hold you here, root and all, in my hand,
Little flower—but if I could understand
What you are, root and all, and all in all,
I should know what God and man is.

There is a great deal of difference in the two poems. Tennyson pulled the little flower out, "root and all," to look at it analytically, as an adult. Blake absorbed the wild flower's presence, more like a child, and let it live. Letting the little flower live is more respectful of life and the Creator's presence in this tiny part of God's creation. It allows the little flower to be alive without why.

CONCLUSION

The result of thinking formally and slowly about a definition for "childhood" has yielded four generalizations. Von Balthasar thought that the fundamental nature of children is found in their wonder at being alive. This promotes gratitude, which is the root of ethics. Adults sometimes forget their formation in deep gratitude, which makes a life flowing from such a source confusing to them and sometimes inexplicable. This also makes it difficult to welcome children . . . and thus difficult to become like them.

The second generalization comes from the historians. They observed that a "child" cannot be a stand-alone concept. Infants are literally unable to stand by themselves and survive.[42] They must be part of a network of care and nourishment to thrive fully as human beings. The primary part of this network is one's parents (or other primary caregivers) and the means of maintaining this relationship is play.

Child psychologists are also very interested in the parent-child relationship. They talk about how the quality of secure and insecure attachment influences relationships throughout one's life.[43] Play, however, is the major constructive ingredient of children's

---

42. This raises the difficulty of the feral child.

The most famous "wild child" was Victor of Aveyron. He lived approximately from 1788–1828 and was named by Jean Marc Gaspar Itard. Itard worked with Victor to see what the child could learn. The method of teaching he developed for this had a great influence on Dr. Maria Montessori in Italy, but his efforts provided little success. Victor never learned how to speak more than a few words. It is not known at what age he was abandoned.

Romulus and Remus, the mythical founders of Rome, were abandoned, legend tells us, as infants and were suckled by a wolf. Most children, however, die without nourishing human companionship, food, and shelter.

In 1970 a child was found in California at the age of 13 years and 7 months. She had been isolated by her family. Genie (her pseudonym) never acquired a first-language.

43. The relationship of secure, non-anxious attachment and insecure, anxious attachment to adult life and the church was explored theologically in Berryman, *Children and the Theologians*, 215–223.

relationships. It does not create bonding by itself, but the play of parents (or other primary caregivers) and children influences the quality of the attachment. Play is also used by psychologists to diagnose what has gone wrong in child development and is used to help children and adults heal and flourish despite this.

The final perspective on childhood came from reflection on our own childhoods. An experience from my childhood was used to illustrate this approach and invite you to reflect on your own past. Such stories, despite the vagaries of memory, help us recover the experience of the original unity of life and death and our participation in that unity.

When we integrate these four concepts into a single definition, we get something like this: *Children are grateful for life, relational, and develop through play to absorb the world as a whole of which they are a part.* It is this child—discerned by theology, described by history, understood by psychology, and remembered by each of us—who can guide us toward being part of God's kingdom. When we are grateful, relational, playful, and absorb the world as a unity of which we are a part, we can be more mature adults.

When the church relates to children in a consistently warm and attuned way, there is constructive bonding and the community of creativity can flourish. If the church relates to children in an insensitive, interfering, and rejecting way, there is insecure, avoidant attachment. When the relationship with children is sometimes warm and responsive and other times rejecting, there is insecure, ambivalent attachment. Secure attachment fosters faith as the opposite of anxiety, and insecure attachment fosters anxiety.

Insecure-avoidant attachment is related to narcissistic behavior. When the church is concerned about its own self-fulfillment and communicates with emotional detachment, it supports narcissistic behavior in the church, which in turn makes narcissism seem normal in the culture.

Insecure-ambivalent attachment is related to identity diffusion, which continues into adulthood. Kenneth J. Gergan called this "multiphrenia" in *The Saturated Self* (1991). When the church does not know what it is called to do, it contributes to avoidant attachment and multiphrenia, which contributes to this kind of adulthood also being considered normal as post-modernism.

Chapter 1 already anticipated the problem with this definition. It may be generally true, but not every child fits. Mary and Matt, whom we met in chapter 1, were relational, but they were not grateful and they had trouble using play to enhance their development. They absorbed the world of which they were a part, but something went terribly wrong. This means that the literal concept of children, fashioned in this chapter, is not "literally" true, but it will have to do as a doorway into the kingdom. If we adults emphasize the qualities of the child in the definition, we may be more likely to become part of God's kingdom, but we also need to remember that there is much more than this involved in Jesus' aphorism. That is why it is important to think slowly and formally to discover the treasure hidden in those words.

In the next chapter we will think about children figuratively. This will expand the definition of children by meeting textual and living children as parables of action to see what they can teach us about entering, receiving, and being born into God's kingdom. While this chapter moved formally and decisively from what we know about children to what we don't know about kingdom-entry, the next chapter will invite us to wonder our way into God's kingdom, like children.

CHAPTER 3

Imagining Children as Parables

A FIGURATIVE VIEW OF JESUS' SAYING

We turn now to a figurative view of Jesus' saying. "Figurative" is a "grand term," which includes several "neighboring" kinds of language.[1] Denis Donoghue's list from 2014 includes metaphor, simile, metonymy, synecdoche, and irony, but the list has varied across the centuries. We will confine our discussion mostly to metaphors.[2]

---

1. Denis Donoghue, *Metaphor* (Cambridge, MA: Harvard University Press, 2014), 118–142.

2. Christian interpreters of scripture might add both allegory and typology to this list. Allegory extends a metaphor by narrative and typology links events in the Hebrew Scriptures with the New Testament. An example of typology is linking the Binding of Isaac with the stories of Holy Week and Easter. This might help us see new things in both stories for Jews as well as Christians—things we may like and things we may not like at all! One question this pairing brings up is why God did not allow Abraham to sacrifice his son, Isaac, and yet God sacrificed his own Son, Jesus. Neither the old Christian interpretative categories of "pre-figuring" nor "supersession" are intended here, only similarity and dissimilarity, as with any metaphor's enrichment of reality.

A metaphor is rooted in the plain meaning of the text. This "plain meaning" may not be completely self-evident, as we discussed in the last chapter, but Gertrude Stein (1874–1946) is famous for having urged its importance with her imperial, literary pronouncement, "A rose is a rose is a rose." This bit of dogma inferred that things *are as they are* and that's all that needs to be said. The law of identity holds. Some things, like a rose, are so powerful in their reality that they need no other words to provide additional recognition or appreciation. In other words, the root term, "rose," needs no amplifier to enhance its meaning.[3] The rose is a matter of clear perception, not poetry.

Despite Stein's pontification, a rose's meaning has, indeed, been expanded by the use of metaphors. Robert Burns (1719–1789) compared his beloved to a rose in Scottish dialect. He sang with exuberance: "O my luve's like a red, red rose/ That's newly sprung in June." Both his love and the red rose were enriched in meaning and significance by their comparison, despite being unlike each other in most respects.

What happens if we exchange another word for "rose"? Will the actual flower still smell as sweet? Yes and no . . . The connection between language and what it refers to is mostly a matter of custom, but the custom of the plain meaning can have serious implications. Juliet said from her balcony, "What's in a name? That which we call a rose/ By any other name would smell as sweet." Romeo and Juliet may have been in love no matter what their names were, but the Montagues and

---

3. My words "root term" and "amplifier" are more classically known by the terminology of I. A. Richards as the "tenor," which is the ordinary and expected word, whether it is spoken or not, and the unexpected one, which he called the "vehicle." A metaphor works by "carrying over" (Greek, *metapherein*) the meaning of a word from normal usage to a new one to enrich both.

Capulets maintained the custom of hating each other by the plain meaning of their names. The result was a needless tragedy of literal meaning.

Much thought has been given to the motive for moving beyond the literal. The poet Wallace Stevens (1879–1955) has come about as close as anyone can to saying why we might want to approach Jesus' aphorism figuratively. In *The Necessary Angel: Essays on Reality and the Imagination*, he argues that the use of metaphor is motivated by our "desire for resemblance." A metaphor "enhances the sense of reality, heightens it, intensifies it" by providing a "partial similarity between two dissimilar things." It gives us, as Stevens elegantly suggested, the pleasure of "lentor and solemnity" with respect to the "most commonplace things." By this he meant that even the word "rose" might be expanded in meaning by slowing down our interpretation of it with a surprising, thoughtful, and provoking resemblance to something else, which adds musicality and dignity to its meaning and reality.[4]

In chapter 1 we considered the child/adult paradox and were challenged by its insistence that we need to be fully a child and fully an adult at the same time to be part of the kingdom. In chapter 2 we broke the paradox and focused only on the child to clarify what a child is like. Now we come to the child as a metaphor. Like Burns' love is a rose, so the adult is a child. The "resemblance" in the unlikeness enriches the meaning of both the child and the adult to provide "lentor and solemnity" to becoming part of God's kingdom.

---

4. Wallace Stevens, *The Necessary Angel: Essays on Reality and the Imagination* (New York: Knopf and Random House, Vintage Books, 1951), 77–78. Denis Donoghue discussed Steven's view of resemblance in the chapter "The Motive of Metaphor" of his book *Metaphor*. "Lentor" and "solemnity" are probably musical terms.

In effect, children in this chapter become metaphors as parables of action. They show the resemblance of the creativity in the unlikeness of the adult and the child that is needed for kingdom-entry. First, we will look at the textual children to discover this creativity. In the Gospels we find the silent child in the midst of the disciples, the children in the marketplace calling to each other, and the children in the temple who enthusiastically recognized and named Jesus to the chagrin of the priests. Second, we will participate in the wondering of living children, as they create their interpretations of "The Parable of the Leaven."

THE SILENT CHILD COMMUNICATES BY BEING

> And they came to Capernaum; and when He was in the house he asked them: "What were you arguing about on the way?" But they were silent, for on the way they had argued with one another who was the greatest. He sat down, called the twelve and he said to them "Whoever wants to be first, must be last of all and servant of all."
>
> Then he took a little child and put it among them; and taking it in his arms, he said to them, "Whoever welcomes one such child in my name welcomes me, and whoever welcomes me welcomes not me but the one who sent me." (Mark 9:33–37; Versions of this text may also be found in Matthew 18:1–5 and Luke 9:46–48.)

Why does the text tell us that Jesus put a *non-speaking* child in the midst of the disciples? Did the Gospel writers "forget" to write what the child did, felt, or said? Did they think such things were not worth mentioning? Was the nonverbal communication of the child a random historical artifact or was it an intentional parable? Perhaps the child's silence was a parable of action about the silence of unified knowing, discussed in the last chapter.

Even if the silence of the child is textually ambiguous, there is one certainty about it. It is in sharp contrast to the noisy, wordy, clueless disciples. This striking juxtaposition suggests that there was something significant about the child's silence. What was it? The dramatic contrast arouses our curiosity.

We live in a noisy time, so keeping a silence journal helps us become more conscious of the parable's contrast. We can listen for the silence of children and ask why they are usually presumed to be always noisy, when they aren't. We can likewise presume that the world is always noisy but find that it is not. Noise blatantly obscures silence, but if we learn to listen for silence and value it, we can hear it. Keeping a silence journal will help us understand the child in the midst who challenged the noisy disciples nonverbally.

Both the countryside and the city are noisy but filled with silence. The sounds of crickets chirping, frogs croaking, cattle mooing, and the distinctive rustle of the seasonal wind in the grass and the leaves of trees are the noises in the country, but there are also still nights and times when the moon communicates in silence.

Cities have also been perennially noisy. Think of Rome in the first century, a city of a million people. All night carts banged and clattered over the cobblestones. Drivers shouted and cursed as they drove sweating oxen and braying donkeys to replenish the city's supplies. Jerusalem and other cities must have been the same.

Today we hear cars screeching and trucks growling instead of oxen and heavy carts. We hear horns honking and sirens screaming instead of the drivers shouting at their animals and each other. Today, however, there is a new twist. We use electronic "white noise" or music plugged into our ears to blot out the rest. The silent child communicating in the midst of the disciples stands in stark contrast to all these sounds.

In the parable the child was not the only one who was silent. The disciples also became quiet! They stopped talking when Jesus asked them what they were talking about along the way. The child's silence revealed God's presence, but the silence of the disciples tried to hide their self-centeredness and their loveless lust for power. Their silence shows how sin was present at the beginning of the New Testament as well as the Old Testament. Jesus' male disciples took Adam and Eve's place as the embodiment of turning away from God, while Joseph and Mary listened silently before Joseph did what God said (Matthew 1:18–25) and Mary said, "Let it be" (Luke 1:26–38) to turn toward God.

Children are not always silent about God, but when they begin to talk, we sometimes think they are talking nonsense. This is because they stretch the bits of language they have to approximate what is beyond language. When adults stretch language thin to do this, we call it poetry.

The Welsh physician and poet Henry Vaughn (1621–1695) wrote in "The World":

I saw eternity the other night,
Like a great Ring of pure and endless light,
    All calm, as it was bright;
And round beneath it, Time in hours, days, years,
    Driv'n by the spheres
Like a vast shadow mov'd; in which the world
    And all her train were hurl'd.

Vaughn stretched language to the lean edge of intelligibility, so the immensity of God's eternal presence could seep into us through the thinness of its membrane.

He also subverted language to speak of God with non-sense, like "dazzling darkness" to express what he sensed. Self-contradiction challenges ordinary logic in a way that stretching language thin does not. It disrupts our language habits to leave momentary openings for God to shine through as in Vaughn's "The Night":

> There is in God, some say,
> A deep, but dazzling darkness, as men here
> Say it is late and dusky, because they
>   See not all clear.
> O for that night! Where I in Him
> Might live invisible and dim.

People, including children, stretch and subvert normal language to talk about God because they intuit that God is not a person, place, or thing. Nouns can't name God, as the Jewish Tradition has always known, because God as action and divinity is beyond what a noun can name. Using nouns to speak of God will block the relationship with God as well as frustrate the expression of what one knows about the experience. When we grow lazy with our theological language, it is easy to slip into the fantasy that we can get outside of our relationship with God to speak of the Creator from the "outside," like we talk about tables and chairs while walking around them. When we stop and think, we know this is impossible, because God comes to meet us from beyond, beside, *and* within—all at once, all the time. There is nowhere outside of God, so there is no place to stand outside our relationship with God to observe it from afar, and there is no "thing" there to name.

Young children don't usually make the adult mistake of misplaced concreteness (reification) when they talk about God, because they can't. They have not yet fully objectified the world with language, so they can't talk *about* God until adults teach them how to misspeak. Instead children participate silently in their relationship with God, playing happily like Eileen Elias did in the pear tree at the far end of the garden. We will meet her in the next chapter.

This is not to say that the ability to objectify the world is unimportant. It is very important, because that is how we develop a sense of self and the world, but it is the church's and the family's responsibility to help children continue to respect God's ineffable presence despite this and the importance of silent, absorbing openness to receive it. This kind of knowing is taught above all by example, but there is also a counter-intuitive second step.

We need to give children the gift of classical Christian language to help them create ultimate meaning from what they experience of God's presence. They need to discover the "art of speaking Christian" fluently at an early age when they are attuned to language learning. This seems counter-intuitive for two reasons. First, most people's experience of Christian education involves learning that God is a noun and reducing God's enormous mystery to coloring theological cartoons or seeking God on an electronic screen. The second reason is that many people do not realize how complex this language domain is. They miss the fact that there are four major genres—parables, sacred story, liturgical action, and contemplative silence—that function in different ways to help children make existential meaning.

Fluency in Christian language uses parables, sacred story, and liturgical action to make meaning, but it also keeps the silent knowing of children alive. They learn to use their bodies, minds, and spirits to become mystical theologians if they have the opportunity for regular spiritual practice.[5]

The silent child in the midst of the noisy disciples is not the only child mentioned in the Gospels. Let's also consider the children in the marketplace. These children were calling to each other about games involving dancing and weeping.

A GAME BEYOND DANCING AND WEEPING

"It is like children sitting in the marketplaces and calling to one another, 'We played the flute for you, and you did not dance; we wailed, and you did not morn'" (Matthew 11:16–17). "Yet wisdom is vindicated by her deeds" (Matthew 11:19).

---

5. The knowing of God by contemplative silence has a long history among Christians. It was in the air during Jesus' lifetime. Philo of Alexandria (20 BCE–40 CE), an older contemporary of Jesus, was influenced by Greek philosophy as well as his Jewish heritage in which silent knowing had been practiced since the sixth century before the Christian era. The Jews hid God's name behind the letters YHWH and said "Lord" instead of the name of the Holy One to protect the expansiveness of the experience of the Divine that had made Moses' face glow. The Jews had already discovered with difficulty that the experience of God's silence did not necessarily mean the misery of God's withdrawal. By the time of Philo and Jesus, a blend of Jewish thought with the philosophical speculation of the Greeks about the *Logos* combined to create a mystical theology that would influence Christians and Jews and then, after the seventh century, Muslim mystics.

Diarmaid MacCulloch, whom I am following here, suggested that Philo was well aware that both silence and speech have their own virtue when communicating *with* and *about* the Divine. "Reason might recognize that, in some circumstances where it would be possible to speak, that moment was nevertheless not appropriate." Diarmaid MacCulloch, *Silence: A Christian History* (New York: Penguin Books, 2013), 27–28.

The Jewish Sabbath developed in part as a weekly observance of silence. The Jews also expected that at the end of time ultimate silence would return. In the meantime we usually babble mindlessly like Jesus' disciples, arguing on the way to Capernaum, and those who thousands of years before Christ tried to build the Tower of Babel "with its top in the heavens," to become equal to God through a misuse of language (Genesis 11:1–9).

"They are like children sitting in the marketplace and calling to one another, 'We played the flute for you and you did
not dance; we wailed, and you did not weep'" (Luke 7:32).
"Nevertheless, wisdom is vindicated by all her children"
(Luke 7:35).

Matthew and Luke placed the story of the children in the
marketplace in the context of John's disciples arriving to see
Jesus (Matthew 11:2–19; Luke 7:18–35). This was a serious
and sad occasion. John was in prison and had heard that Jesus
was teaching and proclaiming the kingdom in the cities beyond
the desert. His disciples asked Jesus if he were the one they had
waited for or should they look for another.[6] "Go and tell John
what you hear and see." They had heard Jesus speaking about
the kingdom and they had seen that people were being healed,
so they went away to tell John.

Jesus then turned to those remaining and said, to para-
phrase, that John was more than a prophet, but your generation is different. You are like contrary children in a marketplace
who can't decide what game to play. There is no pleasing you.
John ate no bread and drank no wine and was rejected. He
then referred to himself in the third person. "The Son of Man"
enjoyed table fellowship and drinking wine, but he shared his
table with sinners. You rejected him. You reject the kingdom no
matter who proclaims it!

At first this looks like a simple example story. The adults
of this generation are like indecisive children who can't decide

---

6. Why did John send his disciples to Jesus with this question? All four Gospels report
that John had baptized his cousin Jesus and in that moment he sensed that there was
something special about him. He baptized with water, as he said, but Jesus would baptize
with fire and the Holy Spirit (Matthew 3:11–12; Mark 1:7–8; Luke 3:15–18). The fourth
Gospel tells how John the Baptist specifically called Jesus "the Son of God" (John 1:34).
Perhaps, John needed to be reassured in his perilous situation that the kingdom he had
preached in the wilderness had come or was near (Matthew 3:2).

whether to follow John or Jesus and wind up following neither and losing touch with the kingdom. This interpretation, however, raises some questions.

Matthew and Luke tell us that the children in the marketplace were sitting as they called to each other. Aren't adults the ones who sit in the sun and visit while their children run and play?

There is also something strange about what the children said. Matthew and Luke quoted the children as speaking a single, complex, complaining, adult-like sentence. Is this really the way that children call out to each other when playing or deciding what to play?

What were the games they proposed to play? They have something to do with making music and wailing. Commentators have suggested that the games proposed were "wedding feast" and "funeral," which mimic *adult* activities. This kind of play prepares the young to take on adult roles, but the point here seems to be that the children didn't want to play either game. Why?

Perhaps the most puzzling question is why Jesus would tell an example story about misunderstanding and indecisive adults and infer that they were acting like children? Doesn't this belittle children? His aphorism said we need to be like children to be part of the kingdom. Was there something about the story of the children in the marketplace that Matthew and Luke misunderstood?

The disciples did not always understand Jesus. We just discussed when Jesus put the silent child into the midst of the disciples to teach them about God's kingdom. They thought it worked like an ordinary kingdom, so they were gossiping about who among them would be the most important in its government.

They also misunderstood when Jesus warned them about the teaching and power of the Pharisees and Sadducees. He said, "Watch out, and beware of the yeast of the Pharisees and Sadducees" (Matthew 16:6; Luke 12:1). Jesus was speaking in metaphor, but the disciples took him literally. He asked them, probably with some exasperation, "How could you fail to perceive that I was not speaking about bread? . . . Then they understood that he had not told them to beware of the yeast of bread, but of the teaching of the Pharisees and Sadducees" (Matthew 16:11–12).

There is also something curious about what Matthew wrote after telling this parable. "Yet wisdom is vindicated by her deeds" (Matthew 11:19). Luke ended his story about the children in the marketplace by saying, "Nevertheless, wisdom is vindicated by all her children" (Luke 7:35).

"Vindication" means someone is proven correct after being unjustly accused. Were the children unjustly accused of being indecisive? The vindication might also refer to future generations, looking back. They thought they were wiser because they did follow John and Jesus to find the kingdom. Neither kind of vindication explains why children were used as bad examples instead of good examples of those who show us the kingdom.

Let's try an experiment. What if we remove the-children-in-the-marketplace from its immediate context concerning John's disciples? If we do this there is no need to turn it into an example story. It can be a parable. When this parable is located in the larger context of Jesus' traveling to Jerusalem for the last time—and if we assume that children can show the way to the kingdom—let's ask again why they didn't choose to play either funeral or wedding.

Neither marriage nor funeral seemed right to them because these games are trivial when compared to the kingdom. They are also trivial when compared to where Jesus was going and what he was going to do. The children refused to play either game because they intuited that they were both insignificant when compared to the kingdom, which Jesus would show us in Holy Week and Easter.

The children were holding out for the Easter Game, which integrates the ultimate sadness of Holy Week (the wailing and mourning) and the ultimate happiness and wonder of Easter morning (the happiness of music and dancing) to make Christian joy.[7] This was shown indirectly for the first time in "the parable" of the children in the marketplace, told as Jesus made his way toward Jerusalem.

The joy of Easter encompasses all our tears and laughter,[8] so merely talking about it, like we are doing here, is not nearly

---

7. The complexity of Christian joy needs the whole liturgical year to fully celebrate it, not just Holy Week and Easter. The unified experience of Christmas-Easter-Pentecost is the complete analogue for the Christian approach to life and death. Nicholas of Cusa celebrated this liturgical analogue as the modern era was dawning in the fifteenth century. When his sense of liturgy's relation to reality was lost, Christianity began to neglect its "anchoring" in liturgical action and unintentionally "provoked the iconoclastic counter-movement of modern atheism." Cusanus had developed "an apophatic way of thinking that preempts the nihilistic self-deconstruction of Western Christianity by reconciling the pre-modern synthesis of wisdom and science with the modern ideals of social, political, cultural, and scientific innovation, and the related ideas of individuality and creativity." Johannes Hoff, *The Analogical Turn: Rethinking Modernity with Nicholas of Cusa* (Grand Rapids, MI: Wm. B. Eerdmans Publishing Co., 2013), 24.

8. "Easter joy" and "the whole spectrum of tears and laughter" deserves further comment. I will discuss tears and then laughter with respect to my own work with children. Both tears and laughter are considered to be communication systems that convey meaning without words.

Tears invite distinctions, none of which can exhaust the meaning of this kind of non-verbal communication. In *Crying: The Natural and Cultural History of Tears* (New York: W. W. Norton and Co., 1999), Tom Lutz discussed nine kinds of tears. They flow from pleasure, theological grace, heroism, mourning, revenge, seduction, escape, empathy, and fiction. This list is a bit long. I used a seven-point crying scale with children. There are tears that express what is best about humankind: tears of extreme pleasure, the surprise of God's grace, and the inspiration of heroism. The tears of empathy are neutral, since they echo what is seen and heard. Negative tears flow from pain, mourning, and escape. Tears can be stimulated from present or past experiences, but they can also come from the anticipation of future ones.

enough to truly apprehend it. It needs to be felt in the sorrow and happiness of life and death, in the probing of the children's parable of action, and in the richly nuanced, multi-sensorial liturgical action of Holy Week and Easter.

With these expansive, figurative thoughts, we leave the children in the marketplace, calling to each other, to enter a third text. This time the children are "crying out" in the temple in Jerusalem.

OUT OF THE MOUTHS OF CHILDREN

But when the chief priests and the scribes saw the amazing things that he did, and heard the children crying out in the temple, "Hosanna to the Son of David," they became angry and said to him, "Do you hear what these are saying?" Jesus said to them, "Yes; have you never read,

> "Out of the mouths of infants and nursing babies you have prepared praise for yourself'?" (Matthew 21:15–16)

A group of children saw Jesus walking in the temple and exuberantly greeted him. The priests were "angry" about this, like the disciples were on another occasion. They apparently

---

Laughter can also be divided into a scale to sharpen one's awareness of what it communicates. Perhaps the most complex scale was that of Baldassare Castiglione, who is famous for advising us to do everything with *spezaturra* (graceful ease) in his *Book of the Courtier*, published in 1528, the year before his death. He identified about thirty-five kinds of laughter, illustrated with jokes taken from Cicero. It might be possible to distinguish so many kinds of laughter for a true connoisseur, but only on paper. I divided laughter into seven kinds, as with tears, to help me distinguish the kinds of laughter in a room full of children. My laughter scale, like the crying scale, is divided into three parts. Positive laughter expresses comedy (triumph over adversity, resolution of conflict), mirth (general gladness and merriment), and delight (a specific sense of pleasure and creativity). Neutral laughter comes from tickling and uneasiness. The three negative kinds of laughter are derisive (contempt, ridicule), sardonic (grimly mocking, cynical), and ironic (the opposite of the usual meaning, absurdity).

also wanted to hold the children back and keep them quiet. Jesus, on the other hand, supported the children speaking up! He quoted the Psalms to the priests. The psalmist sang in Psalm 8 how children know things adults don't, so if we listen to them, the glory they chant will strengthen us.

This raises a question for us today. What if our children could learn how to "speak Christian" so fluently that they could express *their own wonder and creativity* in a deeply meaningful way, like the children in the temple did, when they called Jesus the "Son of David"? They knew what to chant, because they had a valid sense of Jesus' presence and were fluent in the language to express it. If our children "spoke Christian" fluently, it would help them be Christian to renew the church as a community of creating.

We turn now to some children learning how to "speak Christian." As with any language, one needs to use it to know it. They are wondering together about "The Parable of the Leaven."

BEING IN PARABLES WITH CHILDREN

There was once someone who said such amazing things and did such wonderful things that people followed him. When they followed him they heard him speaking about a kingdom, but it was not like the kingdom they lived in. It was not like any kingdom they had ever visited. It was not like any kingdom they had ever even heard of. So they just had to ask him, "What is the kingdom of heaven like?"

One time when they asked him that, he said, "The kingdom of heaven is like when a woman takes three measures of flour and mixes them together. She then hid the leaven in the mixture and it was leavened all over."

This is the Godly Play telling of Jesus' parable. It is not a simplified version of "The Leaven." The words are essentially the same, but it is told to children in a circle rather than reading it to them or asking them to read it silently on a page. This approach invites children (and adults) to relax and be open to the parable. Each time it is told, it is like the first time. Each telling is a new invitation to wonder.

But who were the children this was told to? There were 216 of them from five to twelve years of age. They were attending an Episcopal Day School in suburban Houston. Their classes averaged 16.9 members. I was the chaplain of the school and we used an abbreviated version of the Godly Play process[9] to fit into the school's schedule. Six parables were used in the whole study,[10] but what follows involves only the shortest.[11] Let's imagine the children coming into the school chapel from their regular classes. They formed a circle with me on the floor in front of the altar and got ready.

---

9. The Godly Play approach to parables is described in Jerome W. Berryman, *Teaching Godly Play: How to Mentor the Spiritual Development of Children* (Denver, CO: Morehouse Education Resources, 2009), 46–48, 129–140. The whole curriculum is described in the eight volumes of *The Complete Guide to Godly Play* (Denver, CO: Morehouse Education Resources, 2002–2012). This is a spiral curriculum, and the volumes include an overview of the foundational literature for Godly Play as well as a detailed overview of the spiral.

10. This presentation of "The Parable of the Leaven" (Matthew 13:33; Luke 13:20–21) was presented to the boys and girls, who met weekly during the school week for 30 minutes. A total of 89 parable sessions for all ages were involved in the whole study, which resulted in about 44 hours and 30 minutes of audio recordings, which were transcribed. The chapel of the school was used, rather than a classical Godly Play room. This awkward situation showed the flexibility of the Godly Play approach.

11. More information about the actual script and actions for the presentation may be found in Volume 3 of *The Complete Guide to Godly Play* (Jerome W. Berryman, Morehouse Education Resources: CO, 2002, 109–114). This volume includes a discussion about the general approach to parables in Godly Play and includes the lessons that synthesize all of Jesus' parables in the New Testament (Berryman 2002, 77–152).

The Conversation Begins: Wondering About the Basic Metaphor

When the children were settled, I placed a gold box in the middle of the circle. This made the parable the common property of everyone and focused attention on wondering what a parable might be.[12] Why was it in a box?

I picked up the box, turning it this way and that, looking at it with genuine curiosity. "Look, the box is the color gold. There must be something very important inside. Parables are important, so maybe it's a parable. It looks like a present. Parables are presents. They were given to us before we were even born. But look, there's a lid on the box. It's closed. Sometimes it is hard to get inside a parable. You need to be *very* ready. I know what let's do. Let's try." I put the box back on the floor in the middle of the circle, took off the lid, and bent over to look inside.

An eight-year-old responded by saying, "Well, when you said, before we even opened the box, if we try, maybe it will open, but it's just closed right now. Well, that reminds me of the time where the classroom door was closed and everybody was sitting out there for about fifteen minutes. Finally, someone tried the doorknob and it opened."

"It's like you have to find your own way in," another child added.

I took the felt cloth, the "underlay," from the box and spread it out on the floor. "I wonder what *this* could *really* be?" The underlay for "The Leaven" is a tan, rounded triangle about three feet by three feet. It helps the children search for the key metaphor of the

---

12. The whole curriculum is at present being lightly edited to incorporate additional experience with children since its publication and for clarity. These lessons have now been used for over forty years with great success all over the world and in many different languages.

parable.[13] My smoothing out of the underlay was soothing for the group and invested the parable with my love and respect in a tangible way. The children leaned in.[14]

One five-year-old thought the underlay looked like a "golden pot." Another said it was "a triangle with God coming out of it." If you were to read the whole transcript, you might chuckle at some of the responses and dismiss them as uninteresting or unprofitable to reflect on, but I took all the children's responses very seriously to show them that they were in a safe place and that everything they said counted, even their silliest and most obstreperous comments. They were not allowed to mistreat each other, or the parable, but their silliness was treated as raw material to convert into creative depth.

As the children become more trusting and confident, their silliness mostly disappeared, but their divergent thinking expanded. It grew more playfully serious. This showed that their creative process and existential issues had become engaged. The laughter of delight began to dominate their uneasy laughter, which suggested that they were beginning to give birth to important discoveries, even if they didn't *or couldn't* say what their discoveries were.[15]

---

13. The inspiration for language about "being in parables" comes from Dominic Crossan's, *In Parables: The Challenge of the Historical Jesus* (Sonoma, CA: Polebridge Press, 1992). This book was originally published in 1973 by Harper & Row and was part of a line of Crossan's books that began with *Dark Interval* and included *Cliffs of Fall* and *Finding Is the First Act*, which were influential for the development of Godly Play's approach to Jesus' parables.

14. If I had said anything explicitly about an emphasis on feelings or told the children how to think about the parable, I would have intruded on their deepening concentration and their gradual opening to receive the parable *directly*.

15. Reflections on nonverbal communication in Christian language may be found in Jerome W. Berryman, "Laughter, Power, and Motivation in Religious Education" in *Religious Education*, Vol. 93, No. 3 (Summer, 1998), pp. 358–378. This article may also be found in Jerome W. Berryman, *The Search for a Theology of Childhood: Essays by Jerome W. Berryman from 1978–2009*, ed. Brendan Hyde (Ballarat VIC, Australia: Mondotti Press [an Imprint of Connor Court Publishing], 2013), 207–230.

The typists who made the transcripts of these theological conversations all commented on how much laughter there was in the tape recordings. It was infectious, they reported, and they laughed out loud as they typed.

The children continued wondering what a parable might be. Just before they seemed to tire of wondering about the box and the underlay, I paused and then began to present the parable itself.

The Presentation of the Parable

I slowly and meditatively began to tell the parable. There are only about twenty-three words in the typical English translation, but the telling takes longer than one might think because you dwell in each word. The speaking is slow and quiet but the energy in the speaking is active and intense. The goal is to whet the appetite for every word.

As I told the parable, I took the "pieces" of the parable out of the gold box and placed them carefully on the underlay. The woman and a table for mixing the dough were put in the center. The three measures of flour were placed on the symbolic table. I moved my finger around to suggest mixing. A tiny golden triangle was taken out of its ornamented container and "hidden" in the mixture. Another piece, larger than the "mixture" piece, was placed over it to suggest how the mixture swelled up when it was leavened all over. These slow and meditative acts added to the multi-sensorial involvement of the children with the parable. They were invited to enter the parable with their bodies as well as their minds and spirits.

After the parable was presented, the children asked with insistence what the triangle was. I responded, "It's the leaven."

"But what is leaven?"

"What do you think?" They weren't sure.

I added, "I know that what you see is a little, golden triangle, but what could it *really* be? It stands for something. What does it stand for?" The children began to bubble over with ideas, but they went in all directions without a consensus. I finally said, "It's what makes the mixture swell up and get big, but that's not all—is it?"

This conversation neither interpreted "the leaven" nor went outside the parable's metaphor to "explain" it.[16] The door was left open for the children to venture deeper into the parable's core metaphor to continue making more discoveries about the leaven's relation to the parable, to the kingdom, and to them.

Wondering About the Parable

When I finished telling the parable, I sat back, took a deep breath, and invited the children to wonder together about what the parable's "pieces" could *really* be—the woman, the table, the three measures of flour, the mixing movement of the hand, the mixture itself, the swelling piece, and the leaven. The underlay also remained part of the conversation.

A ten-year-old wondered, "So maybe the big thing (the underlay) is the leaven." Another child said, pointing to the underlay, "Maybe that's a giant leaven and it gets stuck in the bread and the woman gets stuck in the leaven, and that means the woman gets stuck in the bread. And they cook it in this giant oven and the

---

16. Discussing things such as baking bread, buying yeast in a store, or how yeast works distracts the children from the metaphorical core of the parable. This also injects the language of history and science into the parabolic language and makes it harder for the children to be "in parables."

There are some practical matters about child development that the experienced storyteller listens for to prevent misunderstandings. Children in early or middle childhood might mistake the term "leaven" for "eleven" or "flour" for "flower." With older children there are more complex questions one needs to be sensitive to. How many parables did Jesus tell about women? Why was the leaven "hidden" in the mixture? What does "leavening all over" really mean? All ages of children seem to enjoy the rhyme of saying "kingdom of heaven" and "leaven" together as they play with the interactions between these two realities.

whole kingdom of heaven is able to eat it." She continued, "The whole people in the kingdom of heaven eat it all. Except the thing is . . . there's only some crumbs . . . like candles on earth, so they all drop 'em down. . . ."

"How big is it gonna get?" another child asked.

A third child responded, "Too big."

I reflected the conversation back to the children, "So the kingdom of heaven is . . . too big?"

They continued, "Yeah, 'cause if you have all those people's souls up there, they've gotta have a lot of room. More people are growing and have more space."

Enthusiasm began to build. Another child said, "Maybe once every year God has someone make a leaven and maybe the leaven somehow has some kind of magical thing in it, like the leaven. (The child pointed at the little golden triangle on the underlay.) Yeah, sort of . . . like power. Has power in it, something magical, some kind of power. . . ."

More children joined in. "Maybe the leaven is the people, and it's like God puts all the people in the bread, and it rises and rises and rises." Someone else said, "The leaven is the people and makes heaven rise and rise." Another child chimed in, "It could be something that has, like loaves of bread that are really, really big. But they're hollow. And so maybe they're hollow inside, but . . . keeps growing 'cause the. . . ." This child's reasoning was stretched beyond the point it could be sustained.

I gently probed, "So the leaven is . . . ?" There was a long pause. A child finally responded, "Maybe Jesus' body." I wondered if that was a thoughtless cliché, parroting what the child had heard during Holy Communion, but his face was so full of delight and discovery that my skepticism dissolved. Whether the words were borrowed or freshly minted, they had became the child's own in that moment. And besides, it's a very creative association at many levels to connect the parable with the Mass, which was something the other children also were intuiting as they wondered about bread.

The Final Step: A Soft Closure

In this abbreviated version of Godly Play, it was now time for a soft closure. A normal session has five parts. Children are welcomed at the threshold of the room and then settled into the circle. Second, the presentation is offered and the children wonder about it. Next they leave the circle to make an art response to the lesson or some personal experience. They also are invited to work with the materials on the shelves. After the work period the children return to the circle for the feast and prayers. Finally, they go out from the room with an affirmation, like the blessing the congregation receives as it leaves the church. As you can see, the deep structure of each full session is the same as the Holy Eucharist, but this abbreviation left out the art response and feast, so we moved directly from the wondering to the soft closure.

The reason for a "soft closure" is to help children realize that they can begin their creative wondering about the parable whenever and wherever they like. This is why there was no summing up or nailing down an approved interpretation for the parable. It remained in play. The game was still on.

A hard closure with a single interpretation misleads children about the nature of parables. They don't sum up. They aren't illustrations. They expand the spirituality of those interpreting them, who discover by their wondering that the parable overflows with meaning for their lives.

A soft closure also recognizes the nature of religious language. Ian T. Ramsey (1915–1972) in the late 1950s argued that religious language is "odd" as compared to the language of science and the language of every day. It is odd in the sense that its meaning can never be exhausted. Ian Ramsey was Professor of Religion at Oxford and then from 1966 until his death, he was Bishop of Durham. He identified Christian language as a "discernment" that is "not exhausted" by objects in space and time. It always refers to something that is invisible. It gives us life when we use the language appropriately and with skill, or as he said, it gives us "depth."

Like playing any game, this "odd discernment" has rules. The appropriate use of the Christian language game does not result in "bigotry or fanaticism," which worried Ramsey. It invites discovery. There is always "something more" than can be said at any particular moment.[17] A hard closure with a summing up and a final conclusion shuts down this "something more," so it is a misuse of this kind of language.

When school was over, I settled into the quiet of the empty chapel to reflect on what had happened during the classes that day. I asked myself two questions. First, did the children engage the existential limits to their being and knowing with their wondering? Second, did they meet God in the parable and thereby transcend the anxiety caused by their existential limits? These questions need a little introduction, but we will soon return to the children to see how they used the parable to cope with their existential limits and anxiety.

EXISTENTIAL LIMITS AND EXISTENTIAL ANXIETY

Over the last two centuries, people like Søren Kierkegaard (1813–1855) and Gabriel Marcel (1889–1973), among others, have emphasized the importance of engaging our existential

---

17. Ian T. Ramsey, *Religious Language: An Empirical Placing of Theological Phrases* (London: SCM Press, 1957), 15, 47.

limits to become mature human beings. Kierkegaard wrote in *The Concept of Anxiety*, first published in 1844, that people who claim to never have known anxiety about life and death may exist, but the reason they have no anxiety is because they are, as he said, "very spiritless." People with spirit must pass through what he called "the school of possibility," examining all sides to religious questions, before becoming faithful, which is the opposite of being anxious.[18]

There is no escape from existential concerns, because, as Marcel reminded us in *Creative Fidelity*, first published in 1940, there is no "tower" one can climb up to look over the existential boundary to see what is on "the other side."[19] Our anxiety is aroused because we can't see exactly what we need to be afraid of—if anything.

Children, of course, have never heard of Kierkegaard or Marcel, and they would not be interested if they had. The same is true of the psychiatrist Irving Yalom, who found four ultimate concerns appearing time after time in his clinical practice. They were death, aloneness, the need for meaning, and the threat of freedom. This squared with what people like Kierkegaard and Marcel had argued, but Yalom was impatient with and avoided the "impenetrable deep-sounding language" used by philosophers. What he knew was that everyone has existential concerns, so he wanted to help, not just talk about them.[20]

---

18. Søren Kierkegaard, *The Concept of Anxiety: A Simple Psychologically Orienting Deliberation on the Dogmatic Issue of Hereditary Sin* (Princeton, NJ: Princeton University Press, 1980), 157–158.

19. Marcel was quoted and further discussed in Jerome W. Berryman, *The Spiritual Guidance of Children: Montessori, Godly Play, and the Future* (New York: Morehouse Publishing, 2013), 109.

20. Irving Yalom, *Existential Psychotherapy* (New York: Basic Books, 1980), 16.

Mick Cooper surveyed the whole field of existential therapies in 2003 and positioned Yalom in a chapter called "The American Existential-Humanistic Approach: Overcoming a Resistance to Life." He crisply defined Yalom's work as primarily "a therapeutic approach informed by existential concerns."[21] In other words Yalom remained a classical psychiatrist, but he included existential concerns as part of his diagnosis and treatment to yield deep health. Yalom is now Professor Emeritus of Psychiatry at Stanford University School of Medicine, as well as a prolific and widely read author.

Existential philosophy and existential therapy ground Godly Play, but its educational method came primarily from Maria Montessori (1870–1952). Godly Play combines her use of the senses in education and her discovery method with the ancient tradition of *lectio divina*, which advocates dwelling with all the senses in scripture with wonder.[22] Sometimes, however, adults doubt that children have existential concerns, so they think children don't really need to go that deeply into scripture or learn *the art of how to use Christian language*, while learning it, to satisfy their own existential anxiety.

People who work with children in hospitals don't have to be convinced that children worry about the limits to their being and knowing. My colleagues in the Texas Medical Center in Houston, especially at Texas Children's Hospital, from

---

21. Mick Cooper, *Existential Therapies* (London: Sage Publications, 2003), 89.

22. This kind of intensive reading is done out loud so that the words can be "chewed," as the monks described the process in the Middle Ages. Four steps developed over the centuries of usage. They are reading, meditation on the text, prayer, and contemplation of God's presence (*lectio, meditatio, oratio, contemplatio*). The tradition of formal reflection on the text goes back at least to Origen in the third century and was established in the monastic setting at least by the sixth century by St. Benedict. The Carthusian monk Guigo II developed the explicit four-step process in the twelfth century.

1974–1984 were the first to appreciate how Godly Play helps children deal with their anxiety about death, the threat of freedom, their fundamental aloneness, and the need for meaning.[23] Still, we are all anxious at some point. What is the difference between ordinary and existential anxiety?

The poet Christian Wiman, seriously ill with cancer, wrote in 2013 that there is "a distinction to be made between the anxiety of daily existence, which we talk about endlessly, and the anxiety of existence, which we rarely mention at all. The former fritters us into dithering distracted creatures. The latter attests to—and, if attended to— discloses our souls."

---

23. Our existential limits form a metaphorical "box" that "boxes us in." This "box" is defined by a fence of paradoxes. A brief description of each of these paradoxes follows.

One of our limiting paradoxes is death. We are born to die, so we push ourselves to be active in order to defy death. Even though we feel more alive when we are active, we also must rest. Resting is the opposing term of the paradox. It scares us, because repose reminds us of death. This intimate danger causes us to become active again, only to rest once more. Existential anxiety comes from this continuing yes-no, off-on oscillation. Each paradox stimulates the other three.

A second limiting paradox is the threat of freedom. We are relatively free, but our wish to be grounded clashes with the groundlessness experienced in freedom. We move toward freedom until we experience its lack of form and then move away, seeking safety in human structures. These structures then close in on us and feel confining. Groundlessness becomes attractive once more, thus stimulating a renewed hunger for form. We shuttle back and forth between a search for structure and freedom from it. This is how freedom becomes a paradoxical threat rather than the pure openness to choose what is prized.

The third limit is found in the gap between us and what is not-us. Our fundamental aloneness is built into our existence. This conclusion is reasonable. We realize that we cannot sustain life alone. Aloneness is self-conflicting even at the cellular level, but it is also psychologically, socially, and spiritually paradoxical. We wish for contact, for protection, and to be part of a larger whole, but when we move toward inclusion, we recoil, because we don't want to be swallowed up by some larger system or person and disappear. This in turn drives us to seek solitude, and the paradox lives on.

Finally, we are creatures who need meaningful certainty for safety, and yet we are suspicious of it, because we know that we created it. If we are the fallible and changing source of meaning, then how can we count on such meaning to be certain? Despite this nagging doubt, we search for certainty, even absolute certainty, to escape the paradox of meaning, but such certainty is impossible. The flight toward certainty results in the flight away from it. At either extreme the creative process withers, so personal meaning dies, and we enter into this kind of paradoxical oscillation between the need for meaning and the mistrust of it.

Ordinary and existential anxiety can be distinguished, but they are also connected. Our daily anxieties stimulate existential anxiety, which is always hovering in the background, and *vice versa*. When this is realized and squarely faced, Wiman said, we can acquire a lightness, a rightness, and a meaning to our lives that is otherwise impossible. He wrote, "So long as anxiety is merely something to be alleviated, it is not life, or we are not alive enough to experience it as such."[24]

Scott Stossel also addressed the complexity of anxiety in 2013. He examined relevant theories, salient therapies, and his personal anxiety-ridden life to explore "whether anxiety is a medical disease or a spiritual problem, a problem of the body or a problem of the mind." He realized that such questions have a long history, dating "back to the clashes between Hippocrates and Plato and their followers,"[25] but he was not primarily interested in history. It was his own pain, like the pain of the poet Wiman, which pushed him to try to understand anxiety.

Stossel refused to reduce his personal experience of anxiety to deficiencies in serotonin and dopamine or to the excess activity in the amygdala and basal ganglia. He feared that this level of analysis contributes to "trudging along pointlessly toward death in a cold, mechanical, and indifferent universe." This is why he encouraged us to consider that religion, philosophy, and medicine *are all needed* to cope with anxiety.[26] I would only add that this is as true for children as it is for adults.

---

24. Christian Wiman, *My Bright Abyss: Meditation of a Modern Believer* (New York: Farrar, Straus and Giroux, 2013), 94.

25. Scott Stossel, *My Age of Anxiety: Fear, Hope, Dread, and the Search for Peace of Mind* (New York: Alfred A. Knopf, 2014), 53.

26. Ibid., 55.

With these matters in mind, let's rejoin the children, who were wondering about "The Parable of the Leaven." They soon felt comfortable enough to express their existential anxiety *within its metaphor*. Let's begin with the responses of the five-year-olds.

The little ones did not refer directly to any of the four existential limits—death, the need for meaning, aloneness, or the threat of freedom. They also didn't use ultimate language, such as invoking "God," and they did not begin to speak in paradoxes, which often appear when language is pushed to its limits.

The youngest children used what vocabulary they had to probe their ultimate boundaries in a tentative and usually ambiguous way. This is why watching body language at this age is especially important. We need *to see* their struggles, because they can't fully articulate them. By six years of age, however, explicit, existential references and paradoxes began to appear. Many of them were related to the woman in the parable.

A girl in middle childhood, which is about six to nine years of age, told how her mother was pushing her in her stroller when they were both hit by a car. Her mother was hospitalized, which made the event even more distressing because of their separation. Death, the threat of freedom, aloneness, and the need for meaning were all stimulated by this awful event, but she was able to feel and express these overwhelming memories as she wondered in the circle with the children about the parable. The parable, the consistent structure of the process, and having the same trusted storyteller week after week to guide the circle, provided this safety. For children, safety is largely a matter of persons, not things.

Another child about the same age told with wide eyes how a glass shelf broke. It cut her mother, who bled. The memory still made her anxious. She twisted her hands and pulled on strands of hair as she spoke. She told how she had been afraid that her mother would die. She desperately wanted to help her mother, but she was, as she said, "just a kid" and couldn't, which made her even sadder and more scared.

The children continued to give voice to stories directly from their lives, but they also wondered more indirectly about their existential limits and anxiety by means of the parabolic woman. Her presence in the parable opened the way for them to explore their concerns by probing who she really was. Several said the woman was "Jesus' mother." One boy said, "Remember that lady who had a little bit of bread? There was also that man, who said, 'If you give me that little bit of bread and then you shall have plenty and then it overflowed.'" This was probably the child's association of the parable with Elijah being fed by the widow at Zarephath as told in I Kings 17:8–24. The association was beautiful, despite its vagaries about the details.

New ideas hurried around the circle about the woman. They were disjointed at first but all tinged with ultimacy: "Bloody Mary," "God's wife," "God's sister," "God's baby that grew up." Then a child said, "Maybe it's one of us." This suddenly deepened everyone's involvement.

A child, looking around the circle, said, "The woman, maybe it's one of the girls." Another said, "Maybe it's me." Still another suggested to a boy, "Maybe it's you." Someone said, "It has to have very long hair" and laughed. The woman had turned into an "it," as if she were not an ordinary woman at all! She had become some kind of powerful force beyond gender that was not just in the parable but in them as well. This not only provided the strength to talk about difficult things, but it also began the process of discovering the presence of the parable's maker in the parable.

DISCOVERING THE PARABLE-MAKER IN THE PARABLE

So, how do the children discover the creative presence of the maker of the parable through their wondering? Sometimes this begins in an unlikely way. A group of children about ten years old wondered what the bread might really be. The conversation was intense.

"So it's a huge piece of bread," someone said.

Another child followed up, "And you can just take pieces off and when you take that piece off it'll grow back again."

The bread, the woman, and Jesus merged. Another child exclaimed, "Maybe Jesus. He's making bread for all the poor people."

Pointing to the little golden triangle that was the image for the leaven, someone else said, "It looks like a little man."

The conversation moved around the circle. "I think it's like . . . God is the bread, and it's sort of swelling and swelling, and people can eat off it, but then it just keeps on growing on and on and. . . ." The voice trailed off and other children joined in.

"Maybe it's holy."

"Maybe it's the bread that the apostles ate before Jesus died."

Another child added, "The person was baking bread for the Last Supper."

"How could we have it today?" As this child spoke, he pointed to the pieces representing the mixture and the leaven on the parabolic table.

"The bread could be communion bread."

"But more powerful . . . You don't even have to bake it. What did you see? Like there's everlasting love there . . . could be everlasting bread . . . And maybe the everlasting bread makes you remember the everlasting love."

Another child added, "Maybe the everlasting bread and the everlasting love are brothers or something."

I asked, "When you start talking about 'everlasting,' is that a different way to speak?"

"I know, 'cause nothing ever lasts." The child looked worried.

Another child said, "'Cause there's not anything we know about that lasts forever."

"God does," someone said.

"And Jesus."

"Except God." The child who had said "nothing ever lasts" had changed his mind.

The children were wondering about time and the symbolic nature of bread in the parable, which merged with wondering about the bread of Holy Communion. Their language about "huge bread," "God," "Jesus," "everlasting bread," eating and growing again, the "Last Supper," and other less explicit but still ultimate references blended God's presence with eternity and the leavened bread. The bread is alive. It can be eaten and yet it "grows back again." Its holiness blends past, present, and future.

The creativity of the bread and the creativity of the parable's maker also began to merge. The children seemed to sense an "everlasting" someone, living in the parable on the floor in their midst. They expressed a fluidity of time and space *in the parable and in their circle* as they wondered. What emerged was a sense of "everlasting love" in the creative presence they felt in the parable laid out in their midst on the floor.

Even text-bound scholars like Joachim Jeremias (1900–1979) have affirmed Jesus' presence in the text. Jeremias lived in Jerusalem as a child and youth for eight years. He became Professor of New Testament at the University of Gottingen from 1935–1968 and wrote the classic *The Parables of Jesus*. At the beginning of his book he wrote, "We stand right before Jesus when reading his parables."[27]

James Breech added to this idea. In *The Silence of Jesus*, he suggested that the "voice" in the parables is one of unspoken love, which the parables show but do not name. This unspoken love is "a mode of being which is grounded in the superabundant power which engenders or fathers-forth all that is counter, original, spare, strange; and if love is a concept that refers to the capacity to engage voluntarily with the freedom of the actual other, then it can be said that Jesus was . . . the most loving and least sentimental man one could imagine."[28] This view sounds almost like an adult elaboration of what the children intuited from the parable and its maker. They expressed this in their talk about "everlasting love."

The parable's maker is both present in and hidden by the parable, but the children recognized the game of Hide and Seek and enthusiastically joined in. Their puzzled faces, the frowns of concentration, the twisting of doubtful strands of hair, and their expressive feet, wiggling with frustration as well as fun, showed their involvement. They searched for the meaning of the parable and the presence of the parable's maker with enthusiasm. When discoveries were made, the laughter of delight rang out, and smiles knit the circle more tightly together.

---

27. Joachim Jeremias, *The Parables of Jesus*, second revised edition (New York: Charles Scribner's Sons, 1972), 12.

28. James Breech, *The Silence of Jesus: The Authentic Voice of the Historical Man* (Minneapolis, MN: Fortress Press, 1983), 222.

The children sensed the *fundamental* "something more" in the parable, which was its maker. This presence gave them a home where they could rest and flourish, despite the limits to their being and knowing. They had intuited that the existential boundaries to human life are inescapable, but they give us our identity as human beings. They also understood the power of God's love to sustain us, despite those limits, and to help us to transcend them through the Creator's presence in the parable. This is not how the children would put it, but, as you have heard, they have their own ways to express such things in a warm and safe environment with the help of a parable and the Parable-Maker, who created it.

CONCLUSION

This chapter celebrates an expanding sense that children are mystical theologians. The silent child taught about the kingdom by presence, rather than speaking. The children in the marketplace taught about the kingdom by refusing to play the adult games of wedding and funeral, so they could go beyond them to imagine joy that combines their sorrow and happiness. The children in the temple recognized Jesus and called him by his theological name. The living children showed how to be in parables to make existential meaning and come close to the parable's maker. Together, both the textual children and the living children showed how to participate in God's reign, which gives us an unlimited place to live despite our existential limits.

A little over half of the chapter was devoted to living children at play with God. This kind of spiritual guidance is not easy to do, but when it is done well it works and is worth the trouble. It is worth the trouble because the children learn the art of creating existential meaning with Christian language and engaging the fundamental creativity of the Creator. Christian language flowed out from Jesus' life and way of speaking, so it discloses the pathway back into that life, which is ultimately the inner life of God, who formed our identities as creators in the beginning.

In the last chapter we narrowed the meaning of "the child" to a definition. This gave us a way to clarify what the child is like that we need to be like to become part of the kingdom. In this chapter we tried to do the opposite. We tried to present children as parables of action to help us imagine the expansive potential of their theological insight as a way to lead us into God's kingdom. The last chapter was controlled, visual, and text oriented. This chapter was more open, physical, and auditory. The last chapter narrowed consciousness, and this chapter expanded it. The next chapter will be even more expansive.

We have now discussed three viewpoints represented by the *quadriga*—the paradoxical chariot and two of the horses. We have looked at Jesus' aphorism as a paradox, a literal statement, and have appreciated its figurative playfulness. In the next chapter we will use the *mystical* perspective to interpret Jesus' aphorism. It will help us move toward home by bringing the *Creator-creator* affinity implied in Jesus' aphorism more clearly into view.

CHAPTER 4

Exploring the
Creator/creator Affinity

A MYSTICAL VIEW OF JESUS' SAYING

E ileen Elias was close to God. There was an affinity between the Creator and this creative child. She was so close to God that she used to play "noughts and crosses with God" (the x's and o's of Tic-Tac-Toe) in the suburbs of London. One day she was playing in a pear tree at the bottom of the garden. She loved to climb up and look down, changing places with God. When she rejoined her parents, she didn't know what to say when they asked her about what she had been doing.

I never did know how to answer. What *had* I been doing? Dreaming over a pond, watching an underwater world? Climbing a tree and being God? Hiding away in a nowhere-land of red raspberries and green gooseberries? Feeling a touch of the sadness of the world among the broken-pots and ashes of dead fires? How could you tell this to the grown-ups? There simply were not words enough; and if there were they wouldn't understand.[1]

This chapter is about the affinity, the closeness, the friend-ship between the Creator and God's creative creatures. This affinity allows some of us, like Eileen Elias, to appreciate a world in which we can play with God and enjoy a spon-taneous, natural closeness. We will look, first, at the affinity between human and divine creating and then discuss the sci-entific view of creativity's origin. We will then explore how the creative process feels in action by describing its structure, gen-eral characteristics, the feelings it arouses, and its four dimen-sions. Fourthly, we will probe the pervasiveness of the creative process in creation and how we need to be aligned with it. The next step is to suggest that what God creates is creating itself. Finally, we will take a look at the church's calling to be a com-munity of creating.

HUMAN AND DIVINE CREATORS

The Hebrew sages were among the first to put the Creator/creator affinity into words. They told how God created us in "the image and likeness" of the Creator (Genesis 1:26–28). This powerful insight became known in Christian theology as the image of God (*Imago Dei*). Christian, Jewish, and Sufi theologians have discussed this insight for centuries, but young

---

1. Quoted in John Pridmore, *Playing with Icons: The Spirituality of a Recalled Child-hood*. Unpublished mss., 2015, 45. The reference is taken from Eileen Elias' *On Sundays We Wore White: Childhood Reminiscences* (Redhill, Surrey: Love & Malcomson Ltd., 1978) 45–46. The whole of chapter 3 about "Green Places" is relevant.

children live this identity daily though they seldom speak of it. This is why we need to listen more carefully to children, like Eileen, as Jesus suggested.

Sometimes adults lose touch with the mutuality of the affinity. A famous example was Ludwig Feuerbach (1804–1872). He grew up in a devout Lutheran family in Bavaria with a famous jurist father who was overbearing and dictatorial. Young Ludwig was religiously sensitive as a child, and as a youth enrolled to study theology at Heidelberg. It was there that he became so fascinated by Hegel's philosophy that he moved to Berlin the next year to study with the great man himself!

Feuerbach subsequently departed from Hegel's philosophy to develop his own, which featured the idea that God is a projection of human nature onto the screen of the heavens. God did not create us, he said. We created God.

Feuerbach collected his writings into twelve volumes, but the book that made him famous was his *Essence of Christianity*, published in German in 1841. He argued that we are the only creatures who have a religion because, unlike other animals, we can carry on an inner I-Thou relationship with ourselves, which we project as the relationship with God. We also have a "species-consciousness" that allows us to transcend our limited individuality by participating in the unlimited potential of our species. He connected our involvement with the potential of the species to the ideals of Christianity to say that religion is really anthropology.

A key example of Feuerbach's projection idea may be found in chapter 8 of *Essence of Christianity*. He argued that Jesus is really "the nature of the imagination made objective." He went on to say that our ability to conceive of the Second Person of the Trinity only in symbols is not because we are incapable of another kind of description. It is because the

Second Person is in fact already a symbol. Jesus is the symbol for God, which is the result of our need to make God concrete. This need arises because we are "governed and made happy only by images, by sensible representations." Feuerbach used nineteenth century science to turn Christianity into an earth-bound set of ideals.

Karl Barth suggested that Feuerbach's projected "humanity" seems lifeless and unrealistic because it is so abstract. It lacks both a sense of evil and death to give it reality.[2] A "religion" of projected inner dialogue and "species-consciousness" is too thin to sustain the heights and depths of daily life.

Mystical theologians have always worried that our affinity with God can block our awareness of God's affinity with us, as in the case of Feuerbach. In the late fifth century the Pseudo-Dionysius[3] began his *Mystical Theology* with a prayer crafted to frustrate psychological/theological projection by its language. He wrote:

Trinity!! Higher than any being

Any divinity, any goodness!

  Guide of Christians

    In the wisdom of heaven!

---

2. Karl Barth made a careful and fair assessment of Feuerbach in his *Protestant Theology in the Nineteenth Century: Its Background and History*, but this reference is to his "Introductory Essay," which is found in Ludwig Feuerbach, *The Essence of Christianity* (New York: Harper & Brothers Publishers, 1957), x–xxxii.

3. The awkward name of "Pseudo-Dionysius" has been used traditionally because the author's name is unknown. He wrote in the late fifth to early sixth century in what we now call Turkey or Syria, but was named "Pseudo-Dionysius" in the fifteenth century, when it was discovered by internal evidence that he was not Dionysius the Areopagite, who lived in the first century and was mentioned in the Acts of the Apostles.

The Dionysius of Acts was one of those who met with Paul (Acts 17:34) after he spoke, "standing in the middle of the Areopagus," which was a great rock northwest of the Acropolis in Athens, where the courts stood. This Dionysius was probably a judge in the Athenian courts and may later have become a bishop.

Lead us up beyond knowing and light,
  up to the farthest, highest peak
    Of mystic scripture
where the mysteries of God's Word
lie simple, absolute, unchangeable
in the brilliant darkness of a hidden silence.
Amid the deepest shadow
  they pour overwhelming light
  on what is most manifest.
Amid the whole unsensed and unseen
  They completely fill our sightless minds
  With treasures beyond all beauty.[4]

To pray to God, addressed in terms of "brilliant darkness"[5] and one who is "unsensed and unseen," keeps us off balance and opens us to absorb God's presence as we pray. Addressing God as "Trinity" also makes reducing God to a projection difficult, because it acknowledges that God comes to us from beyond, but also from beside us through the scriptures, as Jesus. We not only experience Jesus in the scriptures but can also meet him along any road, like Paul's experience on the road to Damascus, or anywhere else our life takes us. We also know God from within through the Holy Spirit. The church has affirmed this complex psychology of God's self-communication since the fourth century, so it was both psychologically useful and theologically proper for Dionysius to address God in this way.

---

4. This translation was found in Denys Turner, *The Darkness of God: Negativity in Christian Mysticism* (Cambridge: Cambridge University Press, 1995), 21. (MT, 997A-B)

5. "Brilliant darkness" is very much like Henry Vaughn's "dazzling darkness," quoted in chapter 3. They both refer to darkness that is not just full of light but astonishingly bright light.

Still, it is important to probe our side of the affinity with the Creator, as Feuerbach did. To explore this more thoroughly, we will leave behind Feuerbach's nineteenth century science and turn to the science of our time to discuss creativity's origin.

THE SCIENTIFIC ORIGIN OF THE CREATIVE PROCESS

A remarkable group of four artists, such as Dale Chihuly, and ten scientists, including Benoit Mandelbrot who discovered fractals and two Nobel laureates, gathered in Aspen, Colorado, to discuss the origin of creativity.[6] The proceedings were published in *The Origins of Creativity* in 2001. The book was organized around what the group considered the four "central themes of creativity": the creative experience in the arts and sciences, the biological basis of the imagination, the creative powers in relation to the environment, and the mind's perception of patterns.

------

6. The word "to create" did not appear in English until about the fourteenth century. When people in the age of Chaucer first used the word, however, they meant something different than we do. Creating was the province of God. Humans only discovered (uncovered or became aware of) what God had created, like a treasure hidden in a field. For example, as late as the sixteenth century, Michelangelo considered the "creating" of his sculptures as taking away the excess stone to free the figures hidden in the marble. Human creativity in the sense of producing something new did not become common currency until the eighteenth century.

In 1927 Alfred North Whitehead (1861–1947), the son of an Anglican clergyman, coined the term "creativity." Whitehead—a distinguished British mathematician, logician, scientist, and philosopher—used the word in his 1927/28 Gifford Lectures at the University of Edinburgh. His lectures were published as *Process and Reality*, which was his most influential philosophical work.

Whitehead opposed the logical atomism of his former colleague, Bertrand Russell, and argued that while the assumption of scientific materialism is useful for some kinds of problems, it is not decisive for discussing human purpose or to develop an integrated view of human meaning. For these topics one needs to use the concept of process. Objects are important in themselves, of course, but in addition to their own reality they also help us as markers to understand process. Whitehead was interested in the "creative advance into novelty" as the key to philosophical description.

Karl Pfenninger and Valerie Shubik summarized the group's discussions by saying that the origin of creativity is in the brain where "novel contexts and representations that elicit associations with symbols and principles of order" take place. The origin of *this origin* came from the "evolutionary path of simple genetic encoding of circuits and Darwinian selection." Human beings have encouraged this "evolutionary path" by inventing unique cultural practices to support creativity.[7] Pfenninger and Shubik concluded that we could now "move beyond the psychologists' phenomenology of creative behavior to an internally consistent theory founded on natural science."[8]

Nancy C. Andreasen was not at the Aspen meeting, but she too has been interested for many decades in the neurological origin of creativity. She came to neurology by way of a Ph.D. in Renaissance literature,[9] a subject she taught at the university level before becoming a psychiatrist interested in healing people whose creative process was ailing. She wrote, "When the associations flying through the brain self-organize to form a new idea, the result is creativity. But if they either fail to self-organize, or if they self-organize to create an erroneous idea, the result is psychosis."[10] This is abrupt but apt, because when the mood disorders and schizophrenia associated with creativity go wrong, they have unusually high rates of suicide—a tragedy which claimed the great English novelist Virginia Woolf, mentioned in chapter 2.

---

7. Karl H. Pfenninger and Valerie R. Shubik, eds., *The Origins of Creativity* (Oxford, UK: Oxford University Press, 2001), 235–236.

8. Ibid., 235.

9. Her first book was *John Donne: Conservative Revolutionary* (1967).

10. Nancy C. Andreasen, *Creating Brain: The Neuroscience of Genius* (New York: Dana Press, 2005), 102.

Woolf suffered greatly and entered a private hospital several times as she grew older, but she was able to continue to work until her suicide by drowning on March 28, 1941. She was fifty-nine when she wrote to her husband, "Dearest, I feel certain that I am going mad again. I can't go on spoiling your life any longer. I don't think two people could have been happier than we have been. V." Her hat and cane were found on the bank of the Ouse River. Her body was found downstream.

Andreasen's work on creativity and mental illness began in the mid-1970s, not long after she joined the faculty at the Iowa College of Medicine. She studied teachers from the Iowa Writers' Workshop, which gave her an opportunity to work with Kurt Vonnegut, Richard Yates, and John Cheever, as well as twenty-seven other well-known writers.[11] This resulted in *The Broken Brain: The Biological Revolution in Psychiatry* (1983).

She has expanded her interests over the decades to promoting the healthy brain. *The Creating Brain* (2005) bore the subtitle "The Neuroscience of Genius," which is fair since she wrote about many geniuses such as Van Gogh, Leonardo da Vinci, Verrocchio, and Michelangelo, but her book was much more about everyone's healthy brain. This health comes from doing what the brain was created to do—create.

Andreasen concluded her book with about a dozen specific activities to keep our brains open to development and plasticity.[12] This is critical, because the brain develops by adding

---

11. This follows Andreasen's description of her work in "Secrets of the Creative Brain" in *The Atlantic* (July/August 2014), 68. She also described this study in *The Creating Brain* (pp. 94–97), which found that although the authors suffered from mood disorders, she did not find that any of the writers were schizophrenic. She continues to study schizophrenia and creative people who seem to have this disability in their families. Mood disorders come and go, so there are moments of lucidity when the author can carry on sustained work, but unrelenting schizophrenia prevents creative work.

12. Andreasen, *The Creating Brain*, 143–181.

connections between neurons, but it also prunes the connections not used. During childhood the natural emphasis is on connecting neurons, but for adults it becomes pruning them, as we learn how to focus our attention. This is why we all need to keep making new connections to keep our brains healthy.

Alison Gopnik talked about neurons and focus in *The Philosophical Baby* (2009). Her analogy for adults to approximate the wonder and openness of babies is that it might feel something like being on vacation in a fascinating place without an agenda. The abundance of new stimuli overwhelms our ability to focus, so we absorb everything all at once.

A neurologist's view of Jesus' aphorism might be that adults need a healthy dose of being childlike to keep their brains healthy and plastic. We need to help our brains constantly reconfigure their circuits, because, as Andreasen wrote wryly, the "difference between a great writer like Shakespeare and, say, the typical stockbroker is the size and richness of the verbal lexicon in his or her temporal association cortices, as well as the complexity of the cortices' connections with other association regions in the frontal and parietal lobes."[13]

The Aspen conference "demystified creativity" by calling attention to "advances in modern neuroscience."[14] Andreasen went a step beyond this. She called for us to demystify the *science* of creativity. Referring to MRI imaging, she wrote, "Playing word games inside a thumping, screeching hollow tube seems like a far cry from the kind of meandering, spontaneous discovery process that we tend to associate with creativity."[15]

---

13. Andreasen, "Secrets of the Creative Brain," 70.

14. Pfenninger and Shubik, eds., *The Origins of Creativity*, 236.

15. Andreasen, "Secrets," 71–72.

Daniel Siegel has carried forward the work of the Aspen group, Andreasen, and others. His recent *Pocket Guide to Interpersonal Neurobiology* (2012) discussed a "triangle of well-being," which "is a . . . metaphor for the idea that mind, brain, and relationships are each one part of one whole."[16]

He wrote, "The brain is the term for the extended nervous system distributed throughout the whole body." It is "the embodied mechanism" that monitors our flow of energy and information. The mind "is an emergent process that arises from the system of energy and information flow within and between people." Relationships within and between people involve the sharing of the embodied and yet emergent flow of energy and information, which in turn feeds back to adjust the brain's processing and the mind.

What we are calling "the creative process," Siegel called "an emergent process that arises from the system of energy and information flow within and between people." We shall return to Siegel's discussion of this "self-organizing process" in chapter 5, but his work is also relevant to the origin of the creative process itself, which we will return to in the next section.

Theology provides a kind of binocular vision when paired with science to see the depth in the big picture of which Siegel's vision is a part. Physicists also help provide this depth of vision, but we need to describe how the creative process feels in action before turning once more to its larger and pervasive reality.

---

16. Daniel J. Siegel, *Pocket Guide to Interpersonal Neurobiology: An Integrative Handbook of the Mind* (New York: W. W. Norton, Mind Your Brain, Inc., 2012), chapter 4. Siegel used a unique system of pagination involving a number for each chapter, followed by an approximate paragraph number. His reference to chapter 4 would be 4-1 to 4-7.

THE AWARENESS OF THE CREATIVE PROCESS: STRUCTURE, GENERAL CHARACTERISTICS, FEELING, AND THE FOUR DIMENSIONS

The Aspen Group was excited about moving "beyond the psychologists' phenomenology of creative behavior" to mapping the activity of the creative process in the brain. This mapping is critical for promoting better general health and neurological care for those whose brains are injured and need repair. Nevertheless, I would like to go in the opposite direction and focus on the "phenomenology of creative behavior."

My reason for doing this is not very lofty. It is the practical need to describe how the creative process feels in action, because it is broader than usually thought. It is a function of our psycho-social-bio-spiritual wholeness and is related to our lasting happiness and maturity, so we need to sharpen our sense of how this process feels so we can use it better to discover our deep identity and guard against creativity's decay and misuse. This is why I will now describe the following related aspects of the creative process: the structure of creativity's flow, its general characteristics, the feelings it arouses, and its four dimensions.

The Structure

The structure of the creative process feels like shifts of energy in a flowing experience. The shifts are usually called "steps" and have been described in a variety of ways. For example, Silvano Arieti described eight models of creativity used from 1908–1964 in his *Creativity: The Magical Synthesis* (1976). This variety ranged from two steps, diverging and converging, to as many as eight steps. Many people, even those who describe the process in "steps," think that such segmenting obscures the fluidity of the process. I agree, but the purpose for talking about the structure of the process in steps is pragmatic. It helps us orient ourselves in its flow.

Graham Wallas (1858–1932) was an early and influential observer of the creative process. He taught at the London School of Economics from 1895–1923 and published several books about human nature and politics. It was his next to last book, *The Art of Thought* (1926), that we are interested in. He wrote in the "Preface" that his main resource was over forty years watching the creative process in action as a teacher, author, and administrator. These observations were supplemented by reading the accounts of creative people in many different fields.

Wallas' description of the creative process has four steps. First, one prepares by looking consciously "in all directions" for a solution. An incubation period comes next, when one relaxes from working consciously on the problem that has become personally significant. During this step the solution sorts itself out unconsciously. It becomes conscious at the moment of illumination, which is the third step. Verification is the fourth step. It involves consciously testing and developing the idea.

A recent eight-step model may be found in Keith Sawyer's *Explaining Creativity: The Science of Human Innovation*, published in 2012.[17] It elaborates Wallas' four-step process. Sawyer's first step is finding and formulating the problem. The process continues by assembling the knowledge relevant to the problem. Third, a broad range of potentially related information is collected. Fourth, incubation takes place. Fifth, a variety of ideas is generated. Sixth, the ideas are combined in unexpected ways. Seventh, the best ideas are selected by using

---

17. R. Keith Sawyer, *Explaining Creativity: The Science of Human Innovation*, second edition (Oxford, UK: Oxford University Press, 2012), 88–90. Appendix A provides the reader with a chronology of creativity studies from the famous lecture of Henri Poincare in 1913 to the National Science Board report in 2010.

relevant criteria. Finally, the idea is "externalized" in materials and representations.

Most people have felt creativity in action, regardless of the number of steps. Theologians have been interested as well. James E. Loder (1931–2001) was an early advocate for thinking of theological transformation in terms of the creative process. He was both a student and then a professor at Princeton Theological Seminary and published many books, but the one most relevant to our concern here was *The Transforming Moment: Understanding Convictional Experiences* (1982).[18]

The model I use gives special attention to the opening and closing of the process, because my interest is related to the spiritual guidance of children. I am interested in when "the problem" (spiritual identity) awakens us and sets us wondering. Who are we, *really*? This is different from an external problem, such as one assigned to an engineering team to solve in two weeks, but both projects will involve the following five steps if creativity is involved.

Wonder opens the process, which leads to scanning for a new coherence to replace the broken or shattered one. Scanning continues until energy shifts again and the insight emerges. It might take minutes or years to appear, but scanning moves forward relentlessly to renew the lost equilibrium of one's world. When the longed-for insight breaks into consciousness, the scanning comes to an end. Sometimes, as Wallas suggested, we can feel the energy shift before the idea becomes conscious. This is because it has already been roughed in unconsciously as a unified whole before it becomes conscious. Once the insight

---

18. A study of the connection between Loder's work and my use of the creative process in Godly Play, mentioned in chapter 3, may be found in the chapter "The Transforming Moment and Godly Play," in *The Logic of the Spirit in Human Thought and Experience* (Eugene, OR: Pickwick Publications, Wipf and Stock, 2014), 105–130.

becomes conscious, even if in fragmentary form, the energy shifts again to the development of the insight.

Development is the fourth step. We work out the details of the new idea and how it might be applied, even if the "new idea" is a new self or personal vision of the world. This step develops the insight into an appropriate form for one's field of interest, using the field's method and language—such as engineering, poetry, music, law, theology, or medicine. We might also put the insight into the language of everyday, which involves bits and pieces of many formal languages, our region's way of speaking, and our family's unique way of expressing itself.

The fifth step is a soft closure, which allows the "solution" to be integrated with the self, one's field, or a newly discovered field in a useful way that can be communicated. The integration of the soft closure continues until anomalies appear and we begin to wonder about the inconsistencies.

The closure needs to be "soft" so the process can open easily when it needs revision. The creator helps the process move forward by steering between chaos and rigidity without losing touch with either openness (that can decay into chaos) or structure (that can decay into rigidity) to maintain the movement of the process to the soft closure.

The General Characteristics

The general experience of the creative process has five characteristics. These are not feelings, which we will come to in a moment. The characteristics are critical indicators that the process is in action.

The characteristics include a sense that the creative process is engaged for itself rather than any product it might produce. Emphasis on the product produces routine work, but usually not something new. A second characteristic is that the creative process is voluntary, so trying to force the process to flow is not likely to be effective. Third, the process involves deep concentration. The fourth characteristic is that time is altered. Sometimes people lose track of time. Things might also speed up because of enthusiasm or go into slow motion as one moves quickly but not in a hurried way. Finally, involvement in the creative process is pleasurable, which means that it is likely to be self-sustaining.

The Feelings Aroused

Wonder is felt when the process opens. This might be caused by a surprise, something overwhelmingly beautiful, or a tragedy that destroys our assumed world. The scanning that comes next seeks to resolve the openness and is felt as curiosity. This curiosity is sometimes mild and sometimes driving, depending on what caused the wonder. This continues until the insight appears, which emerges with a sense of delight. Caring is the next feeling aroused. People often care about their insights and take care to develop them. Closure arouses the feeling of satisfaction from completing the process. This satisfaction adds to the sustaining of the process.

Frustration is also a feeling that is part of the process. It is aroused when the process is blocked. Frustration can overwhelm us and destroy the flow of creativity, but frustration can also push us on to break through it to get the process flowing again. Wonder is the feeling of openness that is the opposite of the blockage that causes frustration.

Wonder not only arises to open or re-open the process. It was also present when the creative process itself was born. The infant is open to everything and full of wonder. Unfortunately, we cannot live in the indeterminacy of perpetual wonder and survive. This is why the creative process is forced to create itself out of what is at hand—the growing brain, emerging mind, and developing relationships. The wonderful, self-organizing process of creativity begins in infancy to regulate what it arises out of. If this self-emergence does not take place, the infant will have great difficulty thriving or even surviving.

As we develop, the creative process divides into four distinct but similar dimensions: creative flow, social play, biological love, and spiritual contemplation. The four dimensions are similar in structure, general characteristics, and feelings aroused. This is because they emerged from a common source, the indeterminate wonder of infants.

Each dimension of the creative process becomes more independent over time, developing its own vocabulary and function. When the four dimensions become integrated consciously later in life, the result is a rich and profound awareness of our fundamental identity as creators.

The Four Dimensions

The four dimensions show a similar structure, corresponding overall characteristics, and comparable feelings. To demonstrate this we will present classical descriptions of each dimension. The descriptions are: Csikszentmihalyi's "flow," Garvey's description of play, St. Paul's poem about love, and Richard of St. Victor's view of contemplation.

In 1990 Mihaly Csikszentmihalyi published a book called *Flow: The Psychology of Optimum Experience*. He provided a book for a general audience with some trepidation, because if its principles were followed, he claimed, people could be truly happy. He cautioned, however, that "a joyful life is an individual creation that cannot be copied from a recipe." There are no easy shortcuts to living creatively.

He also warned in *The Evolving Self: A Psychology for the Third Millennium* (1994) that when people lack the discipline and knowledge to be truly creative, they will try to *simulate* flow by drugs and in other ways. When flow is faked it becomes, as he said, "wasteful or destructive, and in such cases, the result of seeking enjoyment is entropy, a winding down into despair, rather than harmony."[19] The danger of misuse is a concern for all four dimensions of the creative process.

He called the experience that produced deeply satisfying happiness "flow," because so many of the creative people he and his colleagues interviewed talked about the sensation of flowing when there was a combination of skill and challenge that pushed but did not overwhelm one. The experience involved deep concentration to the point that one's body and other concerns are no longer noticed. This takes training and skill involving about ten years, but when the activity flows, such as playing the piano or composing, time falls away and the playing is done for its own sake. The sense of creative flow is so close to play that at the beginning of Csikszentmihalyi's research a careful distinction had to be made for research purposes.

The second dimension of the creative process is social play. We often think of creativity as being personal, the work of a lonely genius, but that is not quite true. Howard Gardner wrote in *Creating Minds* that when Csikszentmihalyi asked him, "*Where* is creativity?" the whole field changed for him.[20] Creativity is much more social than we often think.

Creativity involves the "domain," to use Csikszentmihalyi's terminology, which involves a particular kind of language and procedures. It also involves the "field," which is made up of the

---

19. Mihaly Csikszentmihalyi, *The Evolving Self: A Psychology for the Third Millennium* (New York: Harper Perennial, 1993), 197–199.

20. Howard Gardner, *Creating Minds: An Anatomy of Creativity Seen Through the Lives of Freud, Einstein, Picasso, Stravinsky, Eliot, Graham, and Gandhi* (New York: Basic Books, 1993), 37.

gatekeepers to the domain. This leaves only one-third of the process for the individual, who works in a particular domain or sets up a new one.

A playmate is always present, even in the so-called "parallel play" of young children, but our playmate does not need to be another person. In the card game Solitaire, the cards are the other player. When climbing a mountain solo, the other players are the mountain and the weather.

We already mentioned Catherine Garvey's description of play in chapter 2. It provides our classic view of play, which is almost identical to Csikszentmihalyi's description of flow. In the background to her description stands Johan Huizinga's (1872–1945) iconic book *Homo Ludens*. It was first published in Dutch in 1938. Huizinga was a linguist, historian of the Renaissance, cultural critic, and antagonist of the Nazis when they occupied his homeland during World War II. He died in detention in 1945, bearing the full weight of the Nazis' pathological, cultural play.

Huizinga went beyond his functional description of play to claim that we are fundamentally players. We are *homo ludens* (playing people) rather than makers and users of tools (*homo faber)* or primarily reasoning creatures (*homo sapiens).* Huizinga's view of play has often been misunderstood. He argued that play is not an element *within* culture. It *is* culture, which is a more challenging idea and links culture inextricably with the social dimension of the creative process.

The third dimension of the creative process is love. We also discussed this in chapter 2, when we talked about the Grant Study. George Vaillant wrote eloquently that we need to learn how to not push love away to be mature.[21] We will,

---

21. Vaillant, *Triumphs of Experience*, 50.

however, use a more familiar and poetic vision of love as our classical statement.

Hardly a Christian wedding goes by without reading St. Paul's poem to love (I Corinthians 13), which expresses the hopes of those being married and those remembering their vows. It urges us to think of love as patient, kind, not jealous, not boastful, not arrogant, and not rude. Love is so deeply engaging that it bears, believes, hopes, and endures all things. This is why it lasts forever and has no goal except itself. Jealousy, arrogance, and boasting are not part of love's reality, so people who carry on like this are empty. They are like "a noisy gong or a clanging symbol." This resonates with the descriptions of flow and play.

It may seem odd to make love the biological aspect of the psycho-social-bio-spiritual human being, but that is because its biology has been improperly left out of the discussion. Lewis, Amini, and Lannon wrote in *A General Theory of Love* that, "From the beginning of the twentieth century to its end, influential accounts of love included no biology."[22] This is why they made it their business to add biology to their theory. One of many insights that this generated was how "limbic resonance" makes the match between people while the neocortex makes up reasons why the match is right.[23]

It may also seem strange to use St. Paul's poem as our classical statement of love. Lewis, Amini, and Lannon had something to say about that as well. Poetry is the best way to speak about love, because it connects the limbic system with the neocortex. We need poetry to connect our thinking and emotions

---

22. Thomas Lewis, Fari Amini, and Richard Lannon, *A General Theory of Love* (New York: Random House, 2000), 6.

23. Ibid., 63.

to speak of love.[24] What could be more creative than generating biological children or a relationship that exhibits the love that St. Paul wrote about?

There is something even more fundamentally biological about love. When we look at the systems of the old brain, we find that love gives these primary systems coherence. The primary systems of the old brain are seeking, rage, fear, lust, care, panic/grief, and play.[25]

Love is seeking. It moves toward newness, satisfaction, and creativity, but it is complicated by the rage associated with competing for scarce resources. Fundamental fear in the old brain is not learned. It is a biological alarm system about the danger that accompanies one's seeking. Lust is what pushes us toward creating offspring, but also nonsexual caring for offspring and each other. Panic and grief come from the potential or actual loss of care from loved ones, and finally, play is a way to cope with the conflicts between these primal systems without rage. This fundamental coherence shows the deeply biological character of love, but it also shows from a biological point of view why theologians call love and sin inextricable. We will discuss this in the next chapter.

The fourth dimension of the creative process is contemplation, which is sometimes confused with meditation, but they are not synonyms. Meditation prepares the mind for silent contemplation. One of the ways it does this is by the reflective reading of scripture (*lectio divina*), which is one of the sources for Godly Play, discussed in chapter 3. The mystical theologians

---

24. Robert Frost, for example, wrote that a poem "begins as a lump in the throat, a sense of wrong, a homesickness, a love sickness. It is never a thought to begin with." Quoted without a source in Ibid., 34. The source is a letter from Robert Frost to Louis Untermeyer (January 1, 1916).

25. Jaak Panksepp and Lucy Biven, *The Archeology of the Mind: Neuroevolutionary Origins of Human Emotions* (New York: W. W. Norton & Company, 2012), 32–38.

taught us that meditation helps people relax, gather energy, and expand their capacity for self-giving love (*caritas*) to prepare for contemplation.[26]

The Latin word *contemplatio* was used to translate the Greek *theoria*, which indicated the state of "beholding God" in the Eastern Church. This beholding is a wordless movement of the creative process that begins with wonder's quiet opening. It then moves into silent scanning for anything to be the equal of God until the senses are cleansed and attuned to God. The "insight" is the nonverbal relaxation into union with the Divine. The nonverbal "development" nourishes and expands this union in tune with its manifold overtones. Beholding is done without any reason, like the rose without why, so if we become conscious that we are contemplating, we can be assured that we are not. It is only after a soft closure that we become conscious of what we have been doing.

The classical description of contemplation we will use comes from a major center for the practice of mystical theology in twelfth century Paris. Richard of St. Victor was the Abbot of the Augustinian Abbey of St. Victor from the year 1162 until his death in 1173. He was also active in the University of Paris and fascinated by the psychology of the religious life. He wrote *The Book of the Twelve Patriarchs* to prepare the reader for contemplation. It was there that he wrote, "Contemplation is the free more penetrating gaze of a mind suspended

---

26. Mystical theology began in the Greek-speaking Eastern Church. Origen (184/5–253/4) was one of the first major figures. We already mentioned Pseudo-Dionysius, but what we did not say was that his influence did not begin in Latin theology until after the ninth century. It was John Cassian (c. 360–435) rather than the Pseudo-Dionysius who brought mystical theology into the Latin West in the fifth century. He lived among the solitaries and groups of men and women already living in the deserts of Egypt in the fourth century. He then journeyed West by way of Constantinople and by 415 had settled near Marseilles in modern France and built the Abbey of St. Victor. The spiritual practice at the Abbey shaped Christian monastic life from then to the present.

with wonder concerning the manifestations of wisdom."[27] We often think of the creative process as something people *do*, but the wordless practice of contemplation shows that the creative process is also something that people *are*.

Each of the four dimensions involves the five-step structure of opening, scanning, insight, development, and soft closure, as well as the five characteristics of being voluntary, done for itself, altering time, involving deep concentration, and being pleasurable. The feelings involved in the process are wonder, curiosity, delight, caring, and satisfaction. When the five steps, general characteristics, and feelings are put together, we find an integrated picture of the four dimensions.

The *opening* of the creative process is identified by wonder and is connected to its giftedness and voluntary aspect, because you cannot compel someone to create fluently, to play with serious delight, to love deeply, or to contemplate. *Scanning* is linked to the characteristic of deep engagement and the searching quality in all four dimensions. Scanning is associated with curiosity. *Insight* is the reward for stubborn and unrelenting scanning with little thought about the ultimate product that might result. The hunger for the insight drives the creator. This feeling keeps the creator open and searching for the insight that emerges. When it emerges, the feeling aroused is delight. *Development* expresses the insights coming from flow, play, love, and contemplation with an appropriate language and method for making the insight intelligible and useful. The insight is developed with care and caring to nourish and organize it. *Closure* brings satisfaction and enables the discovery to be communicated to others. The closure is soft, so that the deep current of the creative process can open easily again as it flows between

27. Richard of St. Victor, *The Twelve Patriarchs; The Mystical Ark; Book Three of the Trinity*, trans. Grover A. Zinn (New York: Paulist Press, 1979), 157.

chaos and rigidity. When anomalies appear, they arouse wonder and the process opens once more. This is how the creative process feels to human beings. We turn now to how this process pervades all of creation.

THE PERVASIVENESS OF CREATIVITY IN CREATION

This brings us back to the big picture and, not surprisingly, we find that the physicists are deeply interested. As they speak their own language and use their own method, we find that surprising words appear and wonderful associations are made with what we are talking about.

In *Science, Order, and Creativity* (second edition, 2000), we find two physicists, the late David Bohm and F. David Peat, proposing that the "generative order" (creativity) "proceeds from an origin in free play which then unfolds into ever more crystallized forms."[28] This can be seen in the work of an artist but also in fractals. They wrote, "This is an assertion of nature's creativity. Each level of organization produces something fundamentally new." There is a connection, it appears, between fractals, the unpredictable events of chaos theory, and "cosmic generativity."

The proceedings from the Interdisciplinary Symposium on Complex Systems held in Prague in 2013 included a section called "Meta-Concepts Background." There we read that while many theories try to reduce theoretical complexity in the case of "the description of the creative process (or divergent thinking) this assumption is not useful. If we want to help user in his creative task, we have to fully respect his nature internal processes and this processes are very **complex, irreducible,**

---

28. David Bohm and F. David Peat, *Science, Order, and Creativity*, second edition (London: Routledge, 2000), chapter 4, "The Generative and the Implicate Order."

and has **fractal character.**[29] (The translation into English is not always perfect.)

The above comments from the scientific community open our minds to return to the theologians of the early church. They proposed that there is a movement of energy within the Holy Trinity that overflows to create and continue creating the creation. They used scripture, reason, tradition, and their personal experience of God's self-communication to come to this conclusion. This theology was called the *perichoresis* (Greek *peri* "around" + *chorein* "to make room for," or "go forward," and "contain") and was emphasized in the Greek-speaking Eastern Church. We experience this overflowing energy from beyond, beside, and within as the flow, play, love, and contemplation of our deep identity when the *Imago Dei* is aligned with the Creator, creating.

Gregory of Nazianzus in the fourth century and Maximus the Confessor in the seventh century are examples of those who connected the dynamic relationships within the Holy Trinity with the inner life of the human being. In our time Hans Urs von Balthasar and Henri de Lubac also discussed God's inner, creative energy as related to our own ability to create, but the most important yet down-to-earth place where this is communicated every day is in the celebration of the Holy Eucharist.

The Mass celebrates the Creator/creator affinity through gestures, words, symbols, and community in a way that roughly parallels the structure of the creative process.[30] It invites participants to join in this redemptive process, which is the process

---

29. *ISCS 2013: Interdisciplinary Symposium on Complex Systems*, eds. Ali Sanayei, Ivan Zelinka, and Otto E. Rossler (Berlin: Springer-Verlag, 2014), 170.

30. Opening of the process   Opening prayers
    Scanning   Scripture readings
    Insight   Sermon
    Development   Holy Communion
    Soft Closure   Blessing & dismissal

of re-creation. This re-creation connects and re-connects us to the creativity, which pervades creation and wells up within us.

The creativity that we experience as flow, play, love, and contemplation from beyond, beside, and within is also found in the mineral, plant, and animal kingdoms, but we often miss seeing the process there because it is invisible and because we don't take the time to look for it or have the ability, especially in mathematics, that physicists have to notice it. We missed "seeing" fractals for the same reasons. They were also "invisible" to us, even though they were right before our eyes!

It was difficult to see fractals for at least two millennia because we were enchanted by the power of Euclid's brilliant idea to round off and smooth out nature's roughness to measure the earth (geometry). He managed the earth's irregularity by using ideal figures such as points, lines, triangles, squares, circles, etc. We had to wait to see and accept the repeating patterns in what looked like nature's irregularity until the invention of non-Euclidian geometry and the computer's electronic ability to picture fractals. Euclidian geometry sees the world at rest while non-Euclidian geometry is more interested in the world in action, like the creative process.

Once the idea of fractals was established, we could see them in the branching of trees, the forking of rivers, the complexity of the circulatory system, and the lightning that lights up the skies at night. They were in the spiral patterns of seashells, hurricanes, and galaxies. This dynamic was everywhere! Nature's restlessness and creativity can now be seen in fractals as a beautiful constant.[31]

---

31. Fractals have had a long preparatory history in modern mathematics, but Benoit Mandelbrot (1924–2010) first presented a systematic explanation during lectures in 1973–1974 at College de France. Fractals are now known beyond the world of mathematics, because Mandelbrot and others generated computer pictures of their self-repeating nature. Mandelbrot understood and was appreciative of how this anticipatory creativity produced the discovery so often associated with his name.

Mandelbrot took note of the early intuitions of fractals[32] and devoted a whole chapter in *Fractals* to "Biographical and Historical Sketches."[33] What is most interesting for our purposes is how Christianity pictured patterns of dynamic self-similarity. Perhaps these images were fashioned because of the church's intuitive sensitivity to the creative process in the Mass and all of creation. Recursive figures appeared in illuminated manuscripts, such as the ninth century *Book of Kells*. They are found in the sculptured crosses and other shapes in Aberlemno, Scotland. Repeating patterns appeared in the architectural structure of churches, in the tiles on their floors, and in church furniture. The twelfth century stone pulpit designed by Nicola di Bartolomeo of Foggia for the Ravello Cathedral on the Amalfi Coast is also a good example.

Arthur C. Clarke[34] and others, including Mandelbrot himself, thought these recursive shapes clearly anticipated the discovery of fractals. All I am suggesting, however, is that the repeating patterns in religious art show a sensitivity to the pervasiveness of the creative process in God's creation, which is like the repeating patterns seen in fractals.

Jonathan Swift (1667–1745), Dean of St. Patrick's Anglican Cathedral in Dublin, joked about the repeating nature of creation across many scales in his ironic masterpiece *Gulliver's Travels*, and on a smaller scale in his poem about fleas:

> So, Nat'ralists observe, a Flea
> Hath smaller Fleas that on him prey,

---

32. Benoit B. Mandelbrot, *Fractals: Form, Chance, and Dimension* (San Francisco: W. H. Freeman and Co., 1977), 1.

33. Ibid., 249–274.

34. Arthur C. Clarke is perhaps best known as the writer of the screenplay for *2001: A Space Odyssey*, but his interests also included being an inventor, undersea explorer, and a television host, as well as one of the "Big Three" of science fiction with Robert Heinlein and Isaac Asimov. He moved to Sri Lanka in 1956 and lived there until his death.

And these have smaller Fleas to bite 'em,

And so proceed ad infinitum.

Lewis F. Richardson (1881–1953)—an English mathematician, physicist, meteorologist, psychologist, and pacifist—developed mathematical models of conflict and loved to ask questions no one else thought worth asking. He helped with the discovery of fractals and commented on his model of recursive turbulence in the style of Dean Swift:

Big whorls have little whorls,

That feed on their velocity;

And little whorls have lesser whorls,

And so on to viscosity.[35]

When one zooms in and out of fractals, into little whorls and out into tornados and hurricanes, the same patterns are found, like in the repeating shapes of cauliflower and broccoli florets. My point is that the creative process, which is found everywhere in God's creation and reproduced in the Holy Eucharist and Christian art and architecture, is as pervasive as the dynamic creativity of fractals and is loosely related to them.

Mandelbrot coined the term "fractal" in 1975; in Latin it means "broken."[36] He may not have realized that the *fractus* is a highly significant moment in the Christian Mass. The priest holds up the host (the bread) and breaks it. If the host is a classical one, flat and brittle, the crack can be heard. Life and death are cracked open and then shared in this symbolic way with those who make a small pilgrimage forward to the altar

---

35. Mandelbrot quoted these two poems in *Fractals*, 269. They often appear in this literature such as in Nigel Lesmoir-Gordon, Will Rood, and Ralph Edney, *Fractals: A Graphic Guide* (London: Icon Books, 2009), 33.

36. Benoit B. Mandelbrot, *The Fractalist: Memoir of a Scientific Maverick* (New York: Vintage Books, 2013), 265.

from their seats in the symbolic space of a church, especially in the Catholic, Lutheran, and Anglican traditions. The pilgrims absorb the broken bread and wine into their fractured lives, to be healed by the creative energy of the broken body of Christ and the community gathered to celebrate creation and re-creation in the Holy Eucharist.

The movement of people flowing from the congregation toward the altar and returning in the symbolic space of the church gathers up the dynamic of the creative process within each person, the church, and the movement of the whole creation out from and back to God. At the end of the liturgy, people flow outside the symbolic space to create constructive turbulence in the world around them by promoting the goodness and creativity of God's creation by what they say and how they live.

If we agree about the pervasiveness of the creative process beyond, beside, and within us, then it is important to ask another question: What is it exactly that God creates?

THE CREATING OF CREATING

God creates *creating*. The Creator created creating in us, as the *Imago Dei*, and we create creating in other people, as our part in this flow of the world. God can't be completely reduced to a potter making a pot.[37] God is the invisible activity of the potter's

---

37. Gordon Kaufman (1925–2011) called God "serendipitous creativity" to push back against the anthropomorphisms used to talk about God. His *In Face of Mystery* (1993) was his most sustained argument about God as creativity, but he went beyond this idea to consider God as a *force* working in the cosmos. He then realized that this thought merely replaced a personal agent with an impersonal one. His final conclusion was that creativity "is very close to being a synonym of the concept of mystery." See Kaufman, "On Thinking of God as Serendipitous Creativity" in the *Journal of the American Academy of Religion*, 2001, 412. He also counseled that we cannot wait until creativity is fully understood and formulated by science to understand it. This is because creativity can never be controlled. It is truly a mystery, because of its serendipitous element.

creativity. The potter and the pot are visible evidence of this invisible process. This is why Isaiah warned: "Woe to you who strive with your Maker, earthen vessels with the potter!" (Isaiah 45:9). We are not called to *strive* with but to *cooperate* with God's creativity.

Still, we sometimes feel the urge, as Isaiah acknowledged, to question the Creator. "What are you making"? "Your pot has no handles"? That is when we need to listen again to Isaiah to know that God is hidden and revealed (Isaiah 45:15) in such activity. God is not found in either the rigidity of idols (Isaiah 45:16) or in chaos (Isaiah 45:18). God invites us to make our case and take counsel together (Isaiah 45:21) in community with each other and with the Creator. If we do that with honesty and goodwill, we will discover that the creation is in the "hands" (action) of God, who "stretched out the heavens" and who helps us make pathways straight, to build cities, and to set the exiles free.

Paul acknowledged this when he wrote to the Romans that he and the whole creation were groaning, like women with labor pains, to give birth to "the glory about to be revealed to us" (Romans 8:18–39). The Spirit "intercedes for us with sighs too deep for words." When we are involved in perpetual Nativity "neither death, nor life, nor angels, nor rulers, nor things present, nor things to come, nor powers, nor height, nor depth, nor anything else in all creation, will be able to separate us from the love of God in Christ Jesus our Lord." I would only add, yet once again, that this "love" is broader than we often think. It includes the other three dimensions of the creative process—flow, play, and contemplation. This broader process is at work personally, in the community, and in the cosmos to make a community of creating.

THE COMMUNITY OF CREATING: RELIGION AND SCIENCE

Let's return for a moment to the Aspen conference. It found the scientific origin of creativity in the brain and the brain's evolution, but it had nothing to say about the larger theological picture we have been talking about. Then something curious happened. In the last paragraph of *The Origins of Creativity*, the name Teilhard de Chardin (1881–1955) appeared. Suddenly, the book opened up beyond brains and evolution to the cosmic sense of creativity that Teilhard de Chardin felt in his own life and invited us to notice and care about in the cosmos.

Teilhard de Chardin was a brilliant and creative Jesuit theologian and paleontologist. He lived professionally on both sides of the divide between religion and science, but integrated them personally without confusing them. His scientific field, the science of paleontology, is itself located on a border. It straddles the boundary between biology and geology and takes some 3,000 million years of the earth's pre-history as the object of its study to discover what our origins mean for our lives today.

Teilhard de Chardin never stopped thinking analogically, regardless of which side of the theology-science border he stood. He could not help but live the flow, play, love, and contemplation of the creative process in both domains, because that was his deep identity. His integration of the four dimensions allowed him to make profound contributions to both fields, but it also got him into trouble, which we will come to in a moment.

Teilhard de Chardin expressed his theology in many large-scale and poetic books. He expressed his science in his paleontology expeditions, his numerous papers about fossils, and being part of the discovery of the so-called "Peking Man" (*Homo erectus pekinensis*). But these two habits of mind came together in a little booklet called "The Mass on the World."

He used and worked on this little book all his life, from the horror of the trenches during World War I, where he was a stretcher-bearer and chaplain, to the end of his life in New York City on Easter Sunday in 1955.[38]

I am certainly not the only one to think that this little book was and is significant. Pope John Paul II wrote in 1995 how much "Teilhard's Mass" had meant to him. The occasion was the fiftieth anniversary of the Pope's ordination as a priest. He wrote, "The Mass on the World (is) celebrated in order to offer 'on the altar of the whole earth the world's work and suffering' in the beautiful words of Teilhard de Chardin."[39]

Deep involvement in the Mass enables us, consciously and unconsciously, to align ourselves with the creative grain of the universe and become better scientists and more responsible church members to create a *community* of creating in whatever domain we live and work.

Pierre Teilhard de Chardin thought in terms of stones, fossils, and millions of years, as well as the union of the earth, himself, the church, and God. He did not always have access to the customary symbols for celebrating Holy Communion as he strode out across the deserts of China, sometimes in his cassock and pith helmet, looking for fossils. Nevertheless, he celebrated the Mass daily on the altar of the whole world. It was on *that altar* that he laid the suffering and hopes of humankind in unity with all the profound suffering and happiness that Christ took into himself on the cross to create Easter joy. Each church altar stands for the larger, cosmic altar, like each Sunday is a "little Easter."

The church was not ready for Teilhard de Chardin's cosmic views. It refused to allow the publication of his theological books

---

38. Thomas M. King, SJ, *Teilhard's Mass: Approaches to "The Mass on the World,"* (New York/Mahwah, NJ: Paulist Press, 2005), x–xi. The text of "The Mass on the World" may be found pp. 145–158.

39. Ibid., ix.

until his death in 1955. This is why the words of Pope John Paul II were so important, some forty years later. The church had caught up both personally in the Pope's words and formally among most bishops in the Magisterium, which expresses the authoritative teaching of the Roman Catholic Church.

The integration without confusion of science and religion, which Teilhard de Chardin embodied, is much more likely to be noticed, respected, and lived today because of him. Merely mentioning his name at the end of a creative book about the science of creativity stimulates wonder, which opens the larger sense of what the book's scientific conclusion was about. It allows neighbors in religion and science to reach across the boundary and work together, like Robert Frost (1874–1963) and his neighbor did when they worked on the wall that separated their property at "spring mending-time."

Frost's neighbor muttered the wise aphorism, "Good fences make good neighbors." That's somewhat true, Frost acknowledged in his poem "Mending Wall," but he stressed that, "Before I built a wall I'd ask to know/ What I was walling in or walling out,/ And to whom I was like to give offense./ Something there is that doesn't love a wall."

We need good boundaries to make scientific and theological meaning well, but walls can make enemies as well as friends by their very nature. People practicing religion and science need to gather at the wall to talk back and forth while it is repaired each spring. The danger involved in such a conversation is no greater than the possibility of Frost's apple trees crossing the boundary to eat up the cones under his neighbor's pines.

Ian Barbour, a pioneer in the science-and-religion field, published *Religion and Science*, based on his Gifford Lectures, in 1997. He proposed four ways that science and religion relate to each other. Other typologies have been suggested, but this will do well enough for our purposes here.

Religion and science relate to each other in conflict, which is, indeed, a relationship but an unproductive one, as when fundamentalist biblicists and fundamentalist materialists struggle to defeat each other. A second kind of relationship is independence. The strangers coexist, mostly unknown to each other, at a safe distance or separated by a high wall. There is also the possibility of a relationship of dialogue, such as sharing information and wisdom about life and death back and forth across the boundary. Barbour's fourth type of relationship was the integration of religion and science.

An integration is not a blend. The parts remain independently themselves, but they are put together as equals within a whole. Teilhard de Chardin embodied this in his life, but he was unusual. He did not allow "religion" and "science" to become objective, exterior "things."

Peter Harrison wrote in *The Territories of Science and Religion*, "the 'integration' category is one that applies almost exclusively to the pre-nineteenth century period, when natural philosophy and natural history were closely integrated with natural theology."[40] The objectified, doctrine-bound views of religion and science today began to develop in the seventeenth century. Before that, religion and science were more like habits of mind than terms for entities existing objectively in two different cultures.

In the thirteenth century Thomas Aquinas considered religion (*religio*) a virtue. It was not one of the three theological virtues, rather it was a moral virtue related to justice. *Religio* "refers to interior acts of devotion and prayer," and its interior nature was much more important than any outward expression such as the way we worship, go on pilgrimages, or make

---

40. Peter Harrison, *The Territories of Science and Religion* (Chicago: The University of Chicago Press, 2015), 175.

religious vows.[41] Aquinas also used the word "science" (*scientia*) in his *Summa Theologiae*. *Scientia* referred to "a habit of mind or an 'intellectual virtue.'" Today we are accustomed to thinking of "science" and "religion" as referring to "systems of beliefs and practices, rather than conceiving of them primarily as personal qualities."[42]

The old view of religion and science allowed for an integration like Teilhard de Chardin made (at least by intuition), but this had been forgotten when the church silenced him. Today we subscribe more to "good fences make good neighbors" than integrating the exquisite inner habits of mind that we now call "science" and "religion." These are both beautiful ways of thinking that have become institutionalized in opposition to each other with the sense that you can't belong in both worlds.

The creative process, however, is neither the property of science nor theology, and all those who live in either or both worlds are flawed. We are all limited and sometimes damaged people whose creativity can become sick. We are all in need of re-creation to live in the deep current of the creative process, which is our home.

The church has begun to reach across the wall to shake hands with science, and it has prayerfully revisited the horrors it committed, especially beginning in the seventeenth century, like the burning at the stake of the Dominican friar Giordano Bruno (1548–1600) in Rome's Campo de' Fiori and the house arrest of the elderly and blind Galileo (1564–1642) in his villa at Arcetri near Florence. Redeeming this history can help create creating on both sides of the stone wall at "spring mending time."

Sam Wells, vicar of St. Martin-in-the-Fields, London, is a parish priest, an author, a theologian, and an ethics scholar.

---

41. Ibid., 7.
42. Ibid., 11.

He wrote some years ago, "The power of the church is not that of a parent—greater resources, more experience, greater physical strength; instead, the church's power is that of a child—stubbornness and doggedness, and the tendency to ask awkward or embarrassing questions."[43] The church needs to become like a child to help create a community of creating.

When the church aligns its creativity with that of the Creator, it can become like Eileen Elias when she played with God in the pear tree at the bottom of the garden, or like Albert Schweitzer when he practiced history, theology, music, and medicine in Africa, or like Teilhard de Chardin when he embodied paleontology and the Mass in the Gobi Desert. The church needs to become like a child to be mature beyond the norm.

CONCLUSION

This chapter explored coming close to God and God coming close to us. It discussed the implications of the Creator/creator affinity for creating creativity in the flow, play, love, and contemplation of one another and valuing this deep identity in ourselves. This is possible when we align ourselves with the grain of creating in the cosmos.

An affinity with God evokes our ultimate identity and moves us into the deep current of creativity beyond normal maturity. Maturity beyond the norm, then, is not an end state. It appears when we steer at any age between rigidity and chaos, consciously or unconsciously. Still, this glorious opportunity of living in the deep channel of our true identity can decay into rigidity or chaos at any moment, so we must ask, "How then shall we live." The response to this question is in the next chapter.

43. Samuel Wells, "In an Urban Estate," in *Faithfulness and Fortitude: In Conversation with the Theological Ethics of Stanley Hauerwas*, eds. Mark Thiessen Nation and Samuel Wells (Edinburgh: T and T Clark, 2000), 123.

CHAPTER 5

How Then Shall We Live?

AN ETHICAL VIEW OF JESUS' SAYING

This chapter confronts the decay and disintegration of the four dimensions of the creative process, which frustrates living in the deep channel of our identity as creators. It is about the ethics of living well with the greatest joy despite such decomposition.

We will look first at the link between the ethics of childhood and adults, as Jesus suggested, to understand how they are related. We will then personify this understanding by discussing Thomas Traherne, a poet of childhood and an ethicist for adults. Third, we will go for an imaginary walk with Traherne and Augustine, as they discuss original goodness and original sin. This leads to a discussion about the necessity of engaging evil with the whole person, fully aware of our good and evil tendencies, which is followed by a description about how evil erodes the goodness of creation. We will close by

describing how steering between chaos and rigidity in alignment with the creativity that flows out from and back to God
is the "new idea" about maturity, we set out to find at the
beginning of this book.

CHILDREN'S SPONTANEOUS ETHICS

A one-year-old boy was watching a puppet show. There were
three characters. The puppet in the middle rolled a ball to a
puppet on the right, who rolled it back. The middle puppet
then rolled the ball to the puppet on the left, who ran away
with it. At the end of the show the puppets from the right and
left were set in front of the little boy who had watched all this.
A treat was placed in front of each one. The child was invited
to take a treat away from one of the two puppets. The child
took the treat away from the one who ran away with the ball.
He then leaned over and hit the puppet on the head.[1]

There is significant evidence, like this, to show that young
children are often kind to each other naturally and have a
desire for what is fair. It appears that Wordsworth's "natural
piety," mentioned in chapter 1, has some basis in fact, but evil's
decay of the good in us also comes naturally. Children can be
selfish and even violent, like Mary and Matt, who were also
mentioned in chapter 1. We seem to be a mixture of "original sin" and "original goodness." To find maturity beyond the
norm, we need to connect with our tendency toward original
goodness to counter our tendency toward evil. But what is evil?

Philosophers who talk about evil are committed to a life of
reason, so they find our inclination toward evil embarrassing.
It is irrational and unpredictable. They ask if there is a hidden

---

1. Paul Bloom, *Just Babies: The Origins of Good and Evil* (New York: Crown Publishers, 2013), 7.

reasonableness and goodness to life despite the irrational evil we experience daily. Must we really conclude (rationally) that life is irrational and tends toward evil?

Susan Neiman divided philosophers into three groups. There are those who seek order and reason, despite "brute appearances" (such as Leibniz, Pope, Rousseau, Kant, Hegel, and Marx) and those who think that evil is all there is (such as Bayle, Voltaire, Hume, Sade, and Schopenhauer).[2] Nietzsche and Freud don't fit into either group. They maintained "a sort of heroic scorn" toward wringing one's hands about evil. I would add that children are a fourth group, which Neiman implied.

Children are not interested in good or evil as abstractions. Their questions are direct, especially when they feel safe and respected. "Why *did* Bobbie hit Alice? Why *did* Alice take Bobbie's book? It's not fair." "Why, why, why," they shout! We might say, "That's just the way it is," but that will not end their questions. They have not given up on explanations or their ability to find a better way. They are the "why-group."

From 1974 to 1984 I had an opportunity to listen carefully to adults and children asking ethical questions. Each day during the week I worked in the hospitals of Houston's Texas Medical Center as a medical ethics consultant and teacher, based at The Institute of Religion, which in those days was a four-story building in the center of the campus.

As a lawyer and priest, I listened carefully each morning to adults struggling with medical ethics issues in the hospitals; but in the afternoons, as a Montessori teacher in a Montessori school, I listened just as carefully to children struggling with their ethical problems. On Saturdays my wife Thea and I saw research groups of children in the morning and afternoon to

2. Susan Neiman, *Evil in Modern Thought: An Alternative Story of Philosophy* (Princeton, NJ: Princeton University Press, 2002), 11.

study how to teach them the art of using Christian language to make existential meaning. This later became Godly Play, which was described in chapter 3.

The similarity between the ethics of children and adults became increasingly clear during that decade. It also became clear that being fluent in a language, like that of the Christian People, is important, because it considers ethical questions in the context of one's personal life and death as well as forgiveness and redemption. In addition, the big picture the Christian language entails gives children and adults the perspective to determine what is trivial and what is not in the ethical situation. It also shows where redemption might be found when things go wrong.

As I listened to children on the playground or in the classroom, I heard them say things like: "She didn't mean to." "That's not fair." "No. Don't do that!" "What if I do that back?" "Don't hit." "Stop." "*Now* what are you going to do?" "We need help."

When the children got stuck, I moved casually and quietly beside them and listened for a moment to see if they were going to be able to manage the developing conflict on their own. If not, I made a "time out" sign and waited. If necessary I then put my finger to my lips and said, "Shhh." When they relaxed and stopped talking, I said, "Think."

The next step was to quietly hold out my hands to make a balancing gesture with palms turned up, like a scale weighing both sides. The children understood. I could see them across the playground doing the same thing when they were on their own. The words and gestures made space and time for their creativity to flow again. Conflict breaks out when children (or adults) get stuck in either chaos or rigidity and don't know what to do next—except blame each other and fight.

Most children I worked with were interested in three parts of the ethical situation to decide what is fair. They were curious about the *motive* for the act, the *act* itself, and the *results* of the act. This was interesting, because the same three themes appear in the classical traditions of ethics. Adults talk about the ethics of virtues and character, the ethics of duties and rules, and the ethics of consequences. Children have never heard of these traditions. They just want to keep their games alive, live happily at home together, and make their learning at school more fun.

When children say, "She didn't mean to," they acknowledge the need to take motive into consideration. When they say, "You can't do that" or utter a firm "No," they are focusing on the act itself. When they say, "Now what . . ." they bring the consequences of ethical choices into play. This was their way of deciding what is fair.

By coincidence, during the same decade that I was listening carefully to children and adults talk ethics, psychologists began to experiment with babies and young children to learn more about their moral inclinations. The researchers have been ingenious, as you saw at the beginning of this chapter. *Just Babies: The Origins of Good and Evil* (2013) has summarized this line of empirical studies. The author, Paul Bloom, is a professor at Yale who designs and carries out ethics experiments with babies and young children at The Infant Cognition Center, which was established at Yale University in 1990.

Bloom and his colleagues found that children had "certain moral foundations," which were "not acquired through learning." They don't come from parents, school, or church. They are "instead the products of biological evolution."[3] God laughs and plays! The amoral force of natural selection, it appears,

---

3. Bloom, *Just Babies*, 8.

instills moral thought, and "selfish genes" create altruistic animals. Bloom and others have collected enough evidence to prompt us to patiently and enthusiastically help children make good ethical decisions to support their natural inclinations.

Alison Gopnik made the connection between the philosophical thinking of babies and adults explicit in *The Philosophical Baby* (2009). She teaches in the Department of Psychology and also in the Department of Philosophy at the University of California at Berkeley. Gopnik found that babies think about ethics much like adults do but without our theoretical elaboration. She also connected the ethics of babies with that of adults in another way. The meaning and contentment derived on balance from "the experience of raising children isn't just an evolutionarily determined illusion, like the man in the moon or the terrifying garter snake. Children really do put us in touch with important, real, and universal aspects of the human condition."[4]

Gopnik's comment runs along the same lines as Jesus' aphorism. There is much to be learned from children about being more adult, but many of the great ethicists did not notice how children think about ethics.[5] Gopnik surveyed the *Encyclopedia of Philosophy* from 1967–2009 and found that in 1967 there were no references to children, but by 2009 the *Encyclopedia* had articles about such things as "Infant Cognition" and

---

4. Alison Gopnik, *The Philosophical Baby* (New York, NY: Picador, 2009), 238.

5. *Abelard* (1079–1142), who emphasized the motive in ethics, had a child with Heloise, but they sent the baby away to be raised by Abelard's family. *Jeremy Bentham* (1748–1832), who founded the utilitarian approach to ethics, which focuses on the consequences of one's actions, never married. *Immanuel Kant* (1724–1804), who founded deontological ethics, which focuses on rules and one's duty (*deon*), also never married. Each of these three pioneers in ethics was interested in his emphasis on a single part of the ethical situation as determinant for adult decision-making. *Thomas Traherne* also never married, but he had a unique sensitivity to childhood. *Augustine* lived in a second-class marriage, recognized by Roman law and the church, but he sent his wife back to North Africa from Milan and kept their son, Adeodatus, with him. The boy died as a teenager, not long after he and his father moved back to North Africa. Augustine then remained single the rest of his life.

"The Child's Theory of Mind."[6] The situation is changing in philosophy and theology. As I mentioned earlier, I surveyed six contemporary theologians who are writing significantly about children, but most theologians still remain ambivalent, ambiguous, and indifferent about them.

I would like to mention a few of the philosophers who have given children and ethics some thought. In 1974 Matthew Lipman (1922–2010) published *Harry Stottlemeier's Discovery* for children. Harry's discovery was thinking! Lipman set up the Institute for the Advancement of Philosophy for Children (IAPC) at Montclair State University in Montclair, New Jersey. The IAPC has its own academic journal *Thinking* and has spawned like organizations around the world. Another pioneer in children's philosophy was Gareth Matthews (1929–2011). He published *Philosophy and the Young Child* in 1980, and continued to publish and work in this area until his death. Perhaps, the grandfather of this interest in the ethics of children was G. K. Chesterton (1874–1936). His chapter "The Ethics of Elfland" in *Orthodoxy* (1908) made the case that adult ethics begins with and is connected to the ethics of childhood.[7] Long before Chesterton and the rest, however, there was Thomas Traherne, an Anglican priest from the seventeenth century.

A POET OF CHILDHOOD AND AN ETHICIST FOR ADULTS: THOMAS TRAHERNE

Thomas Traherne (1636/1638–1674) addressed his *Christian Ethicks* to "the curious and unbelieving soul" and assumed the

---

6. Gopnik, *The Philosophical Baby*, 6.

7. Chesterton's "The Ethics of Elfland" is sometimes not taken seriously, but William H. Brenner of Old Dominion University is an exception. His "Chesterton, Wittgenstein and the Foundations of Ethics" may be found in *Philosophical Investigations* 14:4 (October 1991).

irresistible beauty of virtue for adults. His confidence about this beauty was based on what he experienced as a child. This was expressed in his poetry and prose poetry, which needs to be read with his *Christian Ethicks* to fully understand it.

Traherne's poetry may seem naïve and too idealistic today, but he was not unacquainted with grief during his childhood. He lost his mother when young and, perhaps, his father a bit later. He also lived through several sieges of Hereford, his childhood home, by the Parliamentarians ("Roundheads") during the English Civil War (1642–1651). This meant a shortage of food and water, death, sickness, looting, enemy troops in peoples' homes, the desecration of Catholic churches, and carousing in the streets. He was probably a student at Hereford Cathedral School in January of 1649 when King Charles I was beheaded, which was devastating for the Royalists of Hereford. By the time Traherne arrived at Brasenose College, Oxford, at the age of fifteen, he had already seen much trouble.

Traherne wrote later that he wanted to study "felicity" at Brasenose. By "felicity" he meant a wise and lasting happiness. In those days, as in our own time, there was no such course of study offered by the university. Undeterred, Traherne set out after graduation to *educate himself* about the nature of authentic happiness.

Traherne was about twenty years old when he began to serve the rural parish of St. Mary's in Credenhill, five miles northwest of Hereford.[8] He studied felicity by becoming deeply involved in the births, baptisms, marriages, sickness, deaths, celebrations, business decisions, and anxieties of the people in his parish. He also wrote poetry, prose, and many letters to

---

8. Today the village has nearly 4,000 people and the twelfth century St. Mary's church still stands.

friends with whom he shared manuscripts and an interest in the political and theological concerns of the day. As a parish priest, he not only visited the sick and infirmed, but he prayed for and got to know those in the village and surrounding countryside. Most importantly he preached regularly and celebrated the Holy Eucharist at St. Mary's with his congregation.

Traherne's style of poetry may seem at first awkward, as well as naïve and idealistic, but for many today it still remains utterly beautiful and deeply meaningful. However one might feel about his poetry, it laid the foundation for his more academic *Ethicks*, which put his seventeenth century education on display. *Ethicks* was more like spiritual guidance than modern books about ethics. As he said, he did not desire to "stroak and tickle the Fancy." Instead, Traherne wanted to "elevate the Soul, and refine its Apprehensions" in order to make the virtues vividly useful for the journey "to true Felicity, both here and hereafter."

Some also consider Traherne's poetry to be "the first convincing depiction of childhood experience in English literature."[9] In one poem, "Shadows in the Water," we find him playing in a puddle. He saw the sky above reflected in the water, and his feet touched the feet he saw there. "I fancy'd other Feet/ Came mine to touch and meet;/ As by som Puddle I did play/ Another World within it lay." He reached out visually to touch those numinous joys "To which I shall, when that thin Skin/ Is broken, be admitted in."[10]

---

9. Quoted in Graham Dowell, *Enjoying the World: The Rediscovery of Thomas Traherne* (Harrisburg PA: Morehouse Publishing, 1990), 4.

10. We adults trust mirrors to tell us the truth, but children do not always understand mirrors. Traherne seems to be remembering his childhood feelings about seeing himself in a puddle and then playing back and forth with that image as an adult in his poetry. See Umberto Eco, *Kant and the Platypus: Essays on Language and Cognition* (New York: Harcourt, A Harvest Book, 2000), 363–375.

His sharp intellect played back and forth with his imagination. He wrote in "The Salutation" that "From Dust I rise,/ And out of Nothing now awake;/ These Brighter Regions which salute mine Eys, A Gift fro GOD I take,/ The Earth, the Seas, the Light, the Day, the Skies,/ The Sun and Stars are mine if those I prize."[11]

The word "if" in the last line tolls like a great bell. Children may open their eyes with wonder to see beauty in the gift of life, but for many adults a *conscious* choice is needed to open older eyes with wonder to see God's gifts. Traherne's logical argument in *Ethicks* was for those who had lost the ability to naturally prize what God had given them. He knew personally the difficulty of moving from innocence through misery and conflict to grace, so he hoped to open adults to the wonder of God's creation and stir their gratitude for such beauty to make their lives more satisfying.

Traherne was also alert to the dangers of a passive, sentimental theology. He placed one of the few poems he wrote for *Ethicks* in the chapter on "Contentment." He wrote, "Contentment is a sleepy thing!" He did not consider it an end in itself. "Content alone's a dead and silent Stone." His search for lasting happiness and such happiness itself was much more active. "Desire and Love/ Must in the height of all their Rapture move,/ Where there is true Felicity."

Traherne explicitly connected children's spontaneous ethics with adult ethics in "The Return." "To Infancy, O Lord, again I

---

11. Denise Inge suggested that Traherne in some ways anticipated Teilhard de Chardin, "who like Traherne, saw the continuing creative power of God present in the universe." She went on to say that they resonated in ideas such as "Christ is the unifying force of creation, the Alpha and Omega, the head and ruler, the link between all that is divine and human, the eternally creating Word of God." Traherne insisted that "we enter into the heart of the universe" in the cross of Christ. Denise Inge, ed., *Happiness and Holiness: Thomas Traherne and His Writings* (Norwich, UK: Canterbury Press, 2008), 67.

com,/ That I my Manhood may improv;/ My early Tutor is the Womb;/ I still my Cradle lov./ 'Tis strange that I should Wisest be,/ When least I could an Error see."

This was an exceedingly unusual thing for an adult male to write in the seventeenth century—or any century. It came from Traherne's deep confidence in the reality of what Edward Robinson called "the original vision" in his 1977 book by that name. This reality was not something to be "grown out of" but to be returned to for insight and sustenance. It is only today that empirical research, like that summarized in *Just Babies: The Origins of Good and Evil*, shows that Traherne's intuition was substantial (along with Edward Robinson's) about the connection between the morality of children and adults.

When addressing adults, Traherne advocated for virtue/ character ethics. He thought that virtues were habits, but he made clear that they could be either "Virtuous or Vicious" and that for adults the difference is a matter of "Choise and industry." This need for cultivation makes virtues different from a disposition, which is an "inbred Inclination" held from birth. It also differs from a character trait "infused" by God. The virtues were rooted in the rich soil of childhood, but they did not develop well without cultivation. They need to be consciously chosen by adults, loved, *and used* to prove their worth.

Traherne's *Ethicks* developed a long and exquisite catalogue of virtues. He distinguished five major types to give shape to his long list, but his main contribution was the identification of a master virtue, which is gratitude. This was discussed in the last two chapters of *Ethicks* but had already been explored and celebrated in his poetry. Gratitude motivates and gives meaning to the rest of the virtues.

"Gratitude" is the child's intuition of thankfulness for being alive, which is spontaneous. Adults, on the other hand, need to consciously uncover their original gratitude and choose to be alert to its presence, to develop it properly, and to use it well, as with all of the virtues.

Traherne thought that gratitude was the core of the good life, but he did not mean fleeting moments of thankfulness. He meant something more like we find in the words of the Mass he celebrated at least weekly with his parish. The 1661 Prayer Book, which Traherne probably used for the last thirteen years of his short life, said: "It is very meet, right, and our bounden duty, that we should at all times, and in all places, give thanks unto thee, O Lord, Holy Father, Almighty, Everlasting God" (149). When such gratitude is felt with "all the company of heaven," the celebration of Holy Communion focuses one's life, like a magnifying glass focuses the rays of the sun to a sharp point that can kindle fire.

Gratitude is, as the Prayer Book says, a wise custom, ethically just, and eternally true. This is why it is our paradoxical "bounden duty" *to give thanks freely*, which is the only way it can be given truly if we wish to live with felicitous maturity. Adults, however, may sometimes need to begin by giving thanks with conscious intent and effort to recover what they knew as children. This is why the Prayer Book also implies that gratitude is a duty to be exercised, until it can be freely felt, if one seeks the reality of this foundational experience to guide one's life.

Traherne realized that his talk about fundamental gratitude was meaningless to those who had never experienced it or had lost consciousness of it. Skeptics know nothing of this experience, so they doubt the veracity of those, like Traherne, who express deep gratitude from the core of their personality. He said that advising those without this experience is like advising a beggar to give away a kingdom or a dead man to breathe. This is another reason why Traherne's poetry is so important to

understand his ethical thinking. It expresses the emotional reality that prompts the search for mature, rational, ethical behavior, which properly flows from gratitude.

Still, there are those who might be horrified at Traherne's
theology and the feelings underlying it. They might shout,
"Pelagian!" His confidence in virtuous living was what Augustine and the North African bishops condemned in the fifth century and the Roman papacy confirmed. Not everyone agreed
then or now about how drastically sin has marred our ability
to choose what is good, even with God's help. This is such an
important and emotional issue that I would like to approach it
firmly but indirectly. Let's imagine that Traherne and Augustine
go for a walk to discuss this important theological and psychological point.

TRAHERNE AND AUGUSTINE GO FOR A WALK

Traherne loved to walk in the splendor of God's creation. This
is why the intimate Audley Chapel windows, created by Tom
Denny, show Traherne walking, running, and praying in nature.
This treasure of Hereford Cathedral pictures what Traherne
wrote. We do not walk when we move our feet like "logs of wood."
Let's imagine Traherne and Augustine walking and talking in
a relaxed way about human evil in contrast to the goodness of
God's creation.

Christians, since St. Paul, have struggled to understand the
evil they experience personally and in the world around them.
A few Christians have tried without success to transform evil
permanently into good, like the alchemists tried and failed to
turn many kinds of metal into gold. It turns out that evil is
always "there," degrading God's creative goodness by pervert-
ing personal and social good.

To understand how to cope with evil, we need to know it well. Augustine helped enormously when he suggested that evil is not an independent entity locked in a titanic struggle with God. Instead, evil destabilizes the goodness of creation. It is a corrupting force. In our terms, evil degrades the integration of creative flow, social play, biological love, and silent contemplation to erode the goodness of the creative process into chaos or rigidity.

The Hebrew sages of Genesis located the tree of good and evil at the center of the Garden. That is where it really is! Evil is always right in the middle of everything, ruining it, like a rotten apple spoils a barrel of apples that are beautiful, health giving, and delicious.

This is why every generation longs to go back to the dreaming innocence and dependence of Eden before evil. God placed the fierce cherubim and a mysterious flaming sword, turning this way and that, at the eastern boundary of the Garden to keep us out (Genesis 3:24). The tree of life, whose fruit remained unconsumed, was thus protected and has prevailed to give us the ultimate deadline for maturing our creative powers. Both evil and death push us to become authentic creators in God's image *now*! This is not a theoretical situation.

Since evil and death are always with us, they are "original," but so is our freedom and the goodness of creation. Some, like Augustine, have emphasized our continuing incapacity to transform evil into good. He argued that we are unable to do this without God's help, because our reason and will were completely corrupted by the rebellion of Adam and Eve, in whose lives we still participate. Others say that we can work together with God to freely create a better way than falling into evil's decay. These views appear contradictory, but they emphasize two aspects of the same truth. We are an unstable mixture of good and evil.

Traherne emphasized the need to acknowledge freedom and our original goodness so we can choose to love God and each other, as well as to help God create a graceful maturity and community to support it. As Traherne often said, a pool cannot overflow with love for others unless it is over-filled. We are always in need of grace, like a bleeding person needs a continuing transfusion for a wound that won't heal and never will, but redemptive transfusions are gracefully and freely available.

Traherne and Augustine get to know each other as they walk and talk. They realize that there is no clash of temperaments between them. Traherne does not speak for optimists, and Augustine does not speak for pessimists. They are both realists who prize Easter joy. They share the ultimate sorrow and sadness of Good Friday blended with the ultimate happiness and surprise of Easter. This shared experience goes far beyond simple optimism or pessimism.

Traherne agrees with Augustine that we long for home, where our restlessness can rest in God. He also agrees that our personal flaws and the decay of society are too great for the struggle with evil to ever be won. We always need to be healed by God's love, a grace we can never earn. Still, grace can't erase our freedom or we couldn't accept and be grateful for life, which is the root of ethics for children and adults.

They continue their stroll. The caricatures of the centuries fall away and litter the path behind them like discarded masks. As they talk, they realize that their experience with power and its insidious capacity for decay is vastly different. This may have given them different perspectives on power's ability to corrupt.

Traherne was only about twenty years old when he moved to St. Mary's in the village of Credenhill and only about thirty-six when he finished writing his *Ethicks*. He died at an age younger than Augustine was when he became Bishop of the seaport city of Hippo in North Africa. Perhaps Traherne nods his head to acknowledge this difference.

Augustine was forty-one when he became bishop, and he wrote his *Confessions* when he was around forty-three. *Confessions* was the work of a man learning how to be a bishop and arguing for his worthiness to defend the faith. At the end of his life, when he was about seventy-three, he wrote *Reconsiderations*. It was the work of a bishop learning how to be an old man preparing for death, which would come soon in 430. He was still defending his church, which he sometimes confused with himself. He had built a bridge of words between himself and God which he wanted to leave to posterity.

Reconsiderations might be thought of as a second volume to Augustine's *Confessions*. In *Confessions* he told the story up to his baptism by Bishop Ambrose in his thirty-third year, then some thirty years after writing *Confessions* he laboriously reread and commented on the many, large, heavy, handwritten manuscripts stored in his personal library. This was physically difficult for an old man in his early seventies, which was about twice the average life expectancy for his time. This project was also unusual for writers of his era. What it left us was not the living, breathing, controlling, quarrelsome bishop, but "Augustine the author, and that is how he has been known ever since."[12]

Traherne was just beginning to think seriously about political power when he died from smallpox. He had become chaplain in his last years to Sir Orlando Bridgeman, the Lord Keeper of the Great Seal to Charles II, so he was becoming intimately acquainted with political life, as an observer, before he died in Bridgeman's house at Teddington near London. A second

---

12. James J. O'Donnell, *Augustine: A New Biography* (New York: Harper Perennial, 2006), 319.

volume to his *Ethicks*, some thirty years later, would have been interesting and, perhaps, a classic. But it was not to be.

The younger Traherne was mostly innocent of Augustine's direct involvement with power. He bounds along with delight as they walk. The older man, the one of the *Reconsiderations*, probably needs a cane for our imaginary conversation. He walks slowly and carefully to avoid falling, which makes it hard for him to look around to enjoy the beauty of God's creation except when they stop to rest. Still, I can imagine *some* laughter.[13] Perhaps, there was the laughter of recognition about their shared joy as Christians and their common frailty as human beings.

The church has lived with the controversy between Augustine and Pelagius (and stand-ins for Pelagius, like Traherne) for over 1,500 years. Ironically the church is usually Pelagian in its pastoral care and spiritual direction, because those who take responsibility for spiritual guidance need to encourage people to have faith, to love, and to hope, and need a sense that their care makes a difference. It is not surprising to note that Pelagius was primarily a spiritual director.

When the church works for the good of society, it does so with a blend of Pelagian and Augustinian views. It needs to be encouraging to motivate people to help the common good, but this is done with the realization that personally and socially we tend toward evil. This is why strategies for engaging evil and pastoral warnings are so important.

When the church preaches, it is usually Augustinian. Sermons and official statements of the church stress our complete

---

13. This may be a stretch. In *Confessions* Augustine refers to laughter at least seven times, although the index mentions only the time when Augustine and a group of boys stole pears and "giggled." When Augustine reflected on this, he blamed the group for what "he knew" he would not have done alone. His rationale was that one does not usually laugh alone. The times Augustine mentions laughter in addition to the giggling had to do with the laughter of derision. See Henry Chadwick, *Saint Augustine: Confessions*, 6, 33, 48, 52, 83, 109.

dependence on God's grace to cope with the continuing decay of the good within us and in the society around us.

Our unstable mixture of original sin and original goodness forces us to fully engage evil within and around us with the broken wholeness of who we are. We need to be aware of both our Augustinian and Pelagian/Traherne tendencies, because they make up our wholeness, and it is our wholeness that is at stake.

ENGAGING EVIL WITH THE WHOLE PERSON

The history of evil is a long and sad story, but in the eighteenth century a new clarity began to take shape. Natural evil was distinguished from personal evil. The event that crystallized this distinction was the Lisbon earthquake on All Saints' Day in 1755. It destroyed one of the most beautiful, wealthy, and Christian cities in Europe, so many European philosophers and theologians commented on this irony. The consensus called this a natural disaster rather than divine punishment and distinguished its natural cause from the evil that lurks in the human heart.[14]

The next step in the clarification of evil took place during the Second World War and its aftermath. The Holocaust added to

---

14. The earthquake and three following waves of a tsunami took place on All Saint's Day, November 1, 1755. The king and his family survived and left the city. The Prime Minister, Sebastiao de Melo, also survived. When asked what to do, he famously said, "Bury the dead and heal the living" and took charge. The fires were extinguished and the thousands of corpses buried to avoid disease, many being loaded onto barges and buried at sea over the objection of the church. The army was deployed and gallows constructed at high points in the city to deter looters. The army stopped able-bodied people from fleeing the city and forced them to help in the rescue and reconstruction work. This may seem logical to us today, but the prime minister's approach scandalized some of the old nobles and the church. Religious processions and public rites of repentance were needed, they said, not activities ordered by Sebastiao de Melo.

The question that aroused European discussion was whether the disaster ought to be explained by science as a "natural disaster" or must it be called the judgment of God. Nearly every major church, the leading hospital, and a convent were destroyed. Many worshipping Christians were buried in the collapsing churches during Mass. Ironically the red light district was spared. This was the tragedy of the centuries until the Holocaust.

what was discovered during the Lisbon era, because the Holocaust was too complex and horrifying to simply locate in nature or the human heart. The evil that caused the Holocaust was in many ways impersonal, although carried out in very personal ways. It spread throughout networks of ordinary people, who sometimes were not fully conscious of it. This personal and social decay took place under energetic and effective Nazi leadership to be sure, but it was also an unacknowledged drift into evil.[15]

The Holocaust also included the dark side of science. The "final solution" involved "objective" reasoning and the use of the scientific method to create a brilliant and efficient "science of murder."[16] It took a long time to absorb what these two features of evil had to tell us about human nature.

Almost twenty years after the war ended, Hannah Arendt wrote her controversial *Eichmann in Jerusalem: A Report on the Banality of Evil* (1963). She argued that evil was dangerous *because* of its banality. *Anyone* can become evil, even without realizing it, especially under the pervasive control and fear involved in totalitarian rule. Eichmann defended himself at his trial, sitting in a glass box, by citing Immanuel Kant's categorical imperative to do one's duty, as he was ordered to do by the State. He justified his actions by saying that he had merely followed the law and did as good a job at his assigned work as was possible.

Reinhold Niebuhr (1892–1971) had anticipated and warned how personal goodness could crumble under the weight of

---

15. Thomas Harding, *Hanns and Rudolf: The True Story of the German Jew Who Tracked Down and Caught the Kommandant of Auschwitz* (New York: Simon and Schuster, 2013). Lieutenant Hanns Alexander, serving in the British Army, was instrumental in tracking down and arresting Rudolf Hoss, the commandant of Auschwitz. In the eight-page confession, the *Kommandant* of Auschwitz admitted to killing two million people (245), but later in his trial at Nuremburg he claimed that Auschwitz had been a "mistake," but not for moral reasons. It was because the "policy of extermination . . . brought the hatred of the whole world down on Germany" (269).

16. Elie Wiesel, *One Generation After* (New York: Schocken Books, 1965), 16.

systemic, public evil. He published his *Moral Man and Immoral Society* in 1932, when totalitarian rule was on the rise in Europe. Hitler was appointed chancellor the next year. In Russia the intentional and catastrophic famine of 1932–1933 was taking place and the great purges of 1934–1939 were about to begin. Stalin caused the death of more Russian civilians than Hitler killed Jews.

Niebuhr warned how our best ethical impulses can become distorted by society. He attacked our illusions about "doing good" as suffused with hypocrisy and pretense, even if unconscious. Henry Ford's assembly lines were a major target for his concern when he was the pastor of a small, German-speaking congregation in Detroit. The "good" such jobs did to support families dehumanized the workers. In 1928 Niebuhr moved to Union Theological Seminary in New York City to become Professor of Practical Theology and continued speaking out about our sinful nature and moral hope.

Niebuhr taught at Union for almost thirty years, 1928–1960, but the important moment for our interest was in 1939. That was the year Dietrich Bonhoeffer (1906–1945) returned to Union to teach after having been there as a postgraduate student in 1930. He soon decided to return to Germany, leaving on the last scheduled steamer to cross the Atlantic. Once in Germany, he resumed his resistance to Nazi policies as a founding member of the Confessing Church, which had resisted Hitler's manipulation of the church since 1934. As things became more desperate in Nazi Germany, Bonhoeffer became involved in a plot to kill Hitler and was arrested in 1943. He was executed by hanging on April 9, 1945, just two weeks before the Allies liberated the camp where he had been held and only three weeks before Hitler's suicide with Eva Braun in Berlin. Bonhoeffer *was* a moral man in an immoral society, fully aware of his failings and the complexity of the life he had chosen.

Niebuhr understood in general how evil rots the networks of relationships that make up political power, but he also knew firsthand through his relationships with people wielding political power in the United States how individuals can fall prey to the perversion of their highest ideals. His relationship with Bonhoeffer, however, meant that he also knew that it was possible to engage evil with the wholeness of one's flawed being to fight against personal weakness and the complexity of the good's diminishment in society.

Arendt's and Niebuhr's concern about evil did not say much about children, but Elie Wiesel did. He was a Holocaust survivor who tried to keep the enormity of systemic evil intelligible in personal terms to force us to take individual responsibility for it. He refused to use abstractions and demanded that systemic evil be understood specifically in narrative rather than analyzed from afar as a concept. He said that future generations deserved nothing less than *to experience* the Holocaust on a human scale, so he told stories about evil's deceptions and the reality of its decomposition of ordinary people to disclose its power in society.

Wiesel imagined a dialogue with his critics in *One Generation After*:

> *You are not troubled by other people's happiness? Or by the innocence of children?*
> I like happiness and I love children.
>
> *Then why do you tell them sad stories?*
> My stories are not sad. The children will tell you that.
>
> *But they make one cry, don't they?*
> No, they do not make one cry.

Don't tell me they make one laugh!
I won't. I'll only say they make one dream.[17]

Dreaming is like the wonder that opens the creative process. Stories of evil read in safety help children (and adults) create how they will engage evil when they inevitably encounter it in themselves and in others. Children intuitively recoil from the pain and suffering evil causes, small or large, but they need stories to give them the language and alternatives to imagine how justice can be accomplished with caring and courage despite evil. They need to ask questions, be confident in seeking justice, and to use their creativity to find a better way despite the pull of evil's smoothness and shortcuts.

Susan Neiman suggested that people who cooperate to undermine the good are "not mysterious or profound but fully within our grasp." They are like a fungus with shallow roots at the beginning, but a fungus can spread and devastate reality by laying waste to its surface. Evil needs to be confronted when "the roots are shallow enough to pull up."[18] For example, Adolf Eichmann was a vacuum-oil salesman before he became a well-dressed, senior bureaucrat for the "final solution." He did not begin as a monster, but evil thrives on our lack of awareness and grows stronger when we look the other way.

Both Niebuhr and Arendt stand in the Augustinian Tradition, as described by Charles T. Mathewes in his *Evil and the Augustinian Tradition* (2001). Niebuhr emphasized sin as personal decay that expands when co-opted by society's evil, which overwhelms us by the self-contradictions implied in social action. He continuously challenged people in politics to

---

17. Ibid., 76.
18. Neiman, *Evil in Modern Thought*, 303.

be aware of their self-interest and the danger of such things as competing goods and unintended results fostered by their idealism. He wanted people to be realists, but he also warned politicians against becoming cynical and allowing their views to collapse into conservatism. The conservative mentality only reacts to situations instead of engaging events creatively with the wholeness of one's flawed being. Arendt agreed but also stressed the impersonal threat. She thought evil's decay worked unacknowledged in the shadows of political systems, especially totalitarianism, until it was too late to successfully confront it on a personal level.

Niebuhr and Arendt represented the two major parts of Augustine's view of evil, personal perversion and the decay of the public good. With Augustine they challenged people to be careful and realistic about their love. The self-less love of others (*caritas*) can easily decay into selfish love (*cupiditas*), which is blind to justice because it is blind to the needs of others.[19]

Mathewes wrote that together they demanded *acknowledging responsibility for* and *enacting resistance to evil*. They specified and developed these "two core aspects of Augustine's proposed demythologizing response to evil." Niebuhr and Arendt showed how the response to evil "is necessarily both practical and theoretical, as much a moral practice as an intellectual method."[20]

---

19. This stress on love may be more famous in Niebuhr's work, but it is also the foundation of Arendt's scholarly life. Her doctoral dissertation was about love in the work of St. Augustine, written under the direction of Karl Jaspers and the influence of Martin Heidegger. This thesis has been published in English with commentary. See *Hannah Arendt: Love and Saint Augustine*, eds. Joanna Vecchiarelli Scott and Judith Chelius Stark (Chicago: University of Chicago Press, 1996).

20. Charles T. Mathewes, *Evil and the Augustinian Tradition* (Cambridge: Cambridge University Press, 2001), 227.

What children bring to the discussion about evil is a lack of numbness about personal and social pain and a profound disinterest in dramatic abstractions, like "The Third Reich."[21] Evil thrives on abstractions, because few take personal responsibility for their proclamation or resist them until it is too late.

Children are not easily tempted by evil, because they remain in touch with small pleasures as well as their neighbor's pain and the excitement of learning new things about a better way to live. It is hard for evil to erode their goodness, but it is always possible.

The Hitler Youth systematically corrupted many Germans from ten to eighteen years of age, but many children resisted. By 1936 there were over five million children and young people involved, but their attendance was poor at the meetings. In 1939 things became stricter. Belonging to the Hitler Youth was made compulsory, even if parents objected. In 1940 there were eight million children involved and the boys were being trained as soldiers.

As casualties mounted during World War II, the *Hitlerjugend* were sent into battle. The 12th SS Panzer Division fought against British and Canadian forces during the Battle of Normandy with a reputation for fanaticism and ferocity. They were sixteen- to eighteen-year-olds, but there were also ten- and twelve-year-olds who fought in the defense of Berlin. The youth brigade took heavy casualties from the advancing Russians. Only two survived.

---

21. The first Empire (*Reich*) was the Holy Roman Empire (962–1806). The Second Reich was the German Empire (1871–1918). The Third Reich began in 1933 when Hitler was appointed Chancellor and turned Germany into a fascist, totalitarian state that controlled nearly all aspects of people's lives and promoted further evil abstractions such as "the master race" and "the final solution."

HOW EVIL ERODES THE GOOD

Perhaps, the best way to understand evil's erosion of the good is to approach it with narrative rather than analysis, because we get a sense of engaging evil with the whole person. This was the approach of Elie Wiesel, but in this case we will use J. R. R. Tolkien's *The Lord of the Rings*.[22]

Tolkien was a soldier in the trenches of World War I, so he knew overwhelming evil firsthand before becoming an Oxford don, where evil was also present but not on such a dramatic scale. He expressed his personal resistance to evil by writing *The Lord of the Rings*, making evil the main "character" in his story. It is embodied in the Ring, which evokes the lust for power. The story is about people's varied inability to withstand the Ring's malignant potency.[23]

Tolkien focused in depth on the struggles of a few Hobbits who challenged evil. The average Hobbit stands only about three feet, six inches tall. They dress in bright colors and are shy. Hobbits love simple but good food, games, laughter, peace, quiet conversation, and celebration. They love the earth, so they live in burrows. Hobbits' greatest strength is that they are happy. They value wise felicity and have no towering ambitions. They do not relish abstractions. Instead they are personally loyal to each other and to the Shire, where they live. When

---

22. J. R. R. Tolkien, *The Lord of the Rings* (1954; London: HarperCollins, 2004).

23. The Ring was cut from Sauron's hand and lost. It seemed to have a life of its own and corrupted those who wore it. It was found by Deagol whose cousin, Smeagol, killed him for it. Smeagol (later Gollum), who was a Hobbit, lost the ring. Bilbo Baggins, another Hobbit, found the Ring and escaped with it from Gollum. Baggins was able to live fairly well with it without being corrupted. He gave it to Frodo, who carried the Ring to the fires of Mount Doom. Frodo, Sam, and Smeagol/Gollum made that final trip. At the end, as the Ring brought Frodo under its power, Gollum came up from behind and bit off his finger to take back the ring, but Gollum and the Ring fell together into the lava below. The ring and its power were destroyed.

under pressure, however, they can display enormous courage, strength, love, fellowship, and creativity. This is why they could resist the Ring's influence and finally destroy it, but even they needed a bit of luck to accomplish this.

Tolkien vividly described how evil corrupts, both personally and systemically, in his description of Saruman's subtle descent. This began, as evil often does, with good intentions. At first he was eminently wise and was called Saruman the White.[24] He wanted to do good and sought three things to accomplish this: knowledge, organization in the service of knowledge, and control.[25] He felt he needed more power to accomplish his goals, so he got involved with the Dark Lord Sauron, who was prodigiously powerful. As Saruman said, he did this because he could not count on "weak or idle friends."

Saruman's goal was to challenge evil. He thought that since his intent was good, there was no danger of becoming evil himself, like the Dark Lord. He thought he could merely use Sauron's power while he pursued knowledge and organized it for good ends. The need for power, however, slowly dominated his personality, and the decay of his personal goodness inevitably took place. The two figures, Saruman and Sauron, became almost indistinguishable, like their names.

As Saruman was transformed, his manner and voice took on an undefined, absorbing, yet troubling quality. He became *fascinating*, like Hitler and Stalin still are. People felt compelled to listen to him, but they could not remember what he said. All

---

24. Saruman the White was the greatest of the Wise and led the Council for good when *The Lord of the Rings* began. The last time Gandalf, another member of the Council, went to see him, it was clear that Saruman had changed. He had become, as Gandalf said, "Saruman of Many Colours." Saruman could no longer acknowledge his involvement with evil and tried to conceal it from himself and others by his manner and language.

25. Tolkien, *The Lord of the Rings*, 253.

they could remember was that whatever he said seemed wise and reasonable.[26] Saruman became a master of evasion, which induced chaos and rigidity into the lives of his followers and confused them. They lost their balance. In the end, his decay made his self-deception total, and he became a wraith.[27]

The word "wraith" means "ghost" or "spirit." It comes from Scottish dialect, but that meaning is not quite what Tolkien showed in his story about the unreality of evil, despite its power. When Saruman died, those who stood nearby saw a gray mist. It rose slowly to a great height and loomed over the hill like a shrouded, smoky figure. "For a moment it wavered . . . and it bent away, and with a sigh dissolved into nothing."[28]

St. Augustine's famous description of evil was that it is a deprivation of good, a *privatio boni*. Instead of leaving evil at the level of logic and allowing it to get lost in theology books, Tolkien painted us a picture of evil's decay with words, which later became the images of a film. We can see Augustine's *privatio boni* in Saruman's decay, and experience the fear and danger of its corrupting power, while realizing that it is nothing more than a "gray mist" that drifts away into nothing.

Augustine thought that evil was like a tear in a piece of cloth or decay in a tree. The privation is real, but evil is not an independent reality, existing on its own. This is what makes it so difficult to identify, engage, and struggle with. The only way to cope with evil is to keep the goodness of God and God's creation before us as the only true reality, and then challenge the tendency for this goodness to decompose in us and others.

---

26. Ibid., 564.

27. Tom Shippey, *J. R. R. Tolkien: Author of the Century* (New York: Houghton Mifflin, 2002), 127.

28. Tolkien, *The Lord of the Rings*, 997.

It is curious that Tolkien did not tell us much if anything about the Hobbits' religion. Perhaps that would have been pretentious or distracting. Their loyalty and love for each other involved personal creativity, social play, love, and truly beholding others. This was the essence of their religion, along with the liturgy of their small pleasures. Still, there was something very Christian about them.

The author of the second letter to Timothy, writing sometime around the turn of the first century, warned us that evil people and impostors will go on from bad to worse, deceiving others and being deceived. Nevertheless, we are to continue in what we have learned and firmly believed "from childhood" by being acquainted with the sacred writings. These writings teach us how to be grounded and to seek redemption by participation in the reality of Christ's love so we can engage and resist evil's deceptions (2 Timothy 3:13–15).

This brings us once again to Jesus' aphorism as a way of life. It is time to talk more specifically about how to steer between chaos and rigidity at any age from infant to elder. To do this, we will turn to an allegory of life's river and the deep current of creativity within it to see how to resist evil's evaporation of the creative process.

MATURITY BEYOND THE NORM: STEERING BETWEEN CHAOS AND RIGIDITY

The allegory of the river moves from ideas to images, like when John Bunyan (1628–1688) translated theological doctrine into the vivid pictures and wise narrative of The Pilgrim's Progress. The Slough of Despond, the Wicket Gate, and people such as Christian, Pliable, and Obstinate illustrated and organized his theological thought.

Northrop Frye developed a sliding scale for allegory in his classic *Anatomy of Criticism* (1957). At one extreme there is a one-to-one correlation between images and ideas, like in *The Pilgrim's Progress*, which is coherent and invites decoding. At the other extreme, he said, is "the most elusive, anti-explicit and anti-allegorical" poetry you can imagine.[29] Our river allegory is not so much a narrative as it is an organizing image. It invites decoding and, in fact, its ideas will be discussed as we proceed.

The first time I used the metaphor of the river flowing between chaos and rigidity was during the inaugural meeting of the International Association of Children's Spirituality in 2000. This keynote address was published as "The Nonverbal Nature of Spirituality and Religious Language in Spiritual Education" in 2001.[30] This article concluded with a diagram, which organized my thoughts about "the deep channel of living spiritually." I was somewhat tentative about this idea and its diagram then, but now, some sixteen years later, I am much more confident about it. The old form is still there, but new details have been added.

One of the reasons that I am more confident about this image today is because in 2012 Daniel J. Siegel published his *Pocket Guide to Interpersonal Neurobiology* and used a similar metaphor and diagram to illustrate what he calls "interpersonal neurobiology." Siegel conceived of interpersonal neurobiology as the brain, mind, and relationships functioning as an integrated system, as mentioned in the last chapter.

---

29. This follows the discussion of allegory by Northrop Frye in *Anatomy of Criticism* (Princeton, NJ: Princeton University Press, 1957), 89–92.

30. J. Erricker, C. Ota, and C. Erricker, eds., *Spiritual Education: Cultural, Religious and Social Differences; New Perspectives in the 21st Century* (Brighton, UK: Sussex Academic Press, 2001), 9–21. This chapter may also be found in *The Search for a Theology of Childhood: Essays by Jerome W. Berryman from 1978–2009*, ed. Brendan Hyde (Ballarat VIC, Australia: Connor Court Publishing, 2003), 169–186.

Siegel's "river of integration" is bounded on one side by chaos and on the other by rigidity while "harmony runs down the center of the river." He and I both borrowed this image from complexity and chaos theory, which explicates a domain between deterministic order and randomness. The general implications of such thinking for theology and science are interesting and important, but the area of theology especially interested in pursuing this image has been in the field of pastoral care and counseling.

In this book we will think of the river's flow as the creative process. The largest scale for thinking about this deep current is the energy that flows out from and returns to God. The next levels of flow are in the world, then society, the everyday church as the community of creating, and the family. We then come to the flow in each life from birth to death. Within each life there are multitudes of smaller moments of creativity, which follow the same pattern, like Russian dolls. These moments appear fractal-like as the "whorls" of the creative process within the river's turbulence, remembering this as a rough analogy to Lewis F. Richardson's "Big whorls have little whorls,/ That feed on their velocity" mentioned in chapter 4.

Steering and being steered into the deep channel of creativity shows how the child/adult paradox is lived at many levels and personally expresses our gratitude for being alive and our need to be related to others, especially in a community of creating. It is connected to our fundamental nature as playing creatures and our capacity for unitive thinking. Living in the deep channel displays our natural instinct to be mystical theologians, regardless of age and with or without language. It is related to our affinity with the Creator. When we align our deep identity with the creativity that flows out from and back to the Creator, our steering and being steered into our deep identity is made possible. This is despite the tendency for the goodness of living in the deep channel to degrade into the evil of rigidity or chaos. Nativity is stable, always flowing, inviting us to come create, play, love, and contemplate.

The allegory we are using has some resemblance to when Odysseus steered his ship between Scylla (perhaps a rock shoal on the Italian side of the Strait of Messina) and Charybdis (perhaps a giant whirlpool off the coast of Sicily). The difference is that we are not talking about a boat and crew steering between two dangers. We are talking about life itself flowing between its limits. The banks give the river's flow energy, information, and shape, but sometimes the flow also shapes the banks.

Some of the ideas organized by the allegory are depicted below. The "river" flows between the river's banks. They are the

THE INLAND DANGER ZONE:
This is where one can become stuck in chaos, where nothing is serious. Tears and laughter express madness.

ON THE RIVER BANK:
The openness of comedy is defined in opposition to the form of tragedy.

IN THE SHALLOWS OF THE FLOWING RIVER:
Creativity can be to be used for destructive as well as constructive ends.

THE DEEP CURRENT OF THE CREATIVE PROCESS
The creative process is wholly constructive and involves both the openness of comedy *and* the form of tragedy interacting.

The deep current has four dimensions: flow, play love, and contemplation.

The 4 dimensions share 5 characteristics. The process is done for itself.
It is voluntary and involves deep concentration. It alters time, and is pleasurable.

The 5 steps in the process are the circle of: opening, scanning, insight, development and soft closure.

The feelings aroused by the 5 steps are: wonder, curiosity, delight, careful caring, and satisfaction.
Tears and laughter express each step.

THE DEEP CURRENT OF THE CREATIVE PROCESS

IN THE SHALLOWS OF THE FLOWING RIVER:
Creativity can be used for destructive as well as constructive ends.

ON THE RIVER BANK:
The form of tragedy is defined in opposition to the openness of comedy.

THE INLAND DANGER ZONE:
This is where one can become stuck in rigidity, where everything is serious. Tears and laughter express scorn.

boundaries of comedy and tragedy defined in opposition to each other, rather than refreshing each other. These limits are where one could still return to the river and its deep current. We risk not being able to return to the river if we venture very far inland into the chaos of madness or the utter scorn of rigidity.

A living system stores information and yet is flexible enough to communicate, create, and sustain life. Creativity emerges from the interplay of chaos and rigidity in this living system without being overwhelmed by either. This is true for the creativity in all kinds of systems such as physics, cultures, religions, individuals, and Siegel's neurobiology. This is how "creativity creates creating" on all scales, as discussed in the last chapter.

The allegory pictured above shows the flow of maturity beyond the norm, which is the same for children and adults, although adults are usually more conscious of it and can speak about it. Infants and children are more likely to intuit where they are in this picture and communicate their whereabouts with tears and laughter. Maturity beyond the norm flows when freedom (tending toward chaos) is combined with the ability to sustain continuity (tending toward rigidity) without getting stuck in either.

If the creative process drifts over the bank into chaos, it spins apart and dies. If it drifts over the other bank into rigidity, it grinds to a halt, breaks down, and dies. These two kinds of "death" take place, even if the person continues to exist biologically. Being stuck high and dry results in a diminished state, a *privatio boni*, which frustrates the functioning of our deep identity and warns us to steer back into the deep channel.

We sometimes laugh until we cry and cry until we laugh at our tears, so healthy and creative laughter and tears are related. When tragedy and comedy separate and become defined *against each other*, laughter and tears also divide. They no longer refresh each other. We hear all the kinds of laughter in the river. In the deep current we hear the laughter and see the tears that express the feelings in the flow of the creative process—wonder, curiosity, delight, careful caring, and the smile of satisfaction.

When this book began there was talk about the lure of happiness that would lead us to maturity beyond the norm. It did lead us part way home, but on the way we discovered that there is an emotion that is much more related to maturity beyond the norm. It is the mixture of happiness and sadness in Christian joy, which is much more realistic than seeking mere happiness for the long run. We hear the laughter of joy as the river renews itself after flooding over its banks into chaos or rigidity. This is a constant risk, so returning after getting lost is a constant and lovely sound in the river. Evil's decay into chaos or rigidity is always a danger, so a knowing smile expressing the mixture of sorrow and happiness recognizes this reality. The reality of the deep current and the redemption of the return is celebrated in the liturgy of Holy Week and Easter, but also on every Sunday in the year, which is a "little Easter."

Laughter and tears are also our alarm system. They show when the river overflows either bank. The water pools and begins to evaporate along either side. The laughter and tears of disordered madness appear when the river overflows into chaos, where nothing is serious. The laughter and tears of scorn signal when the river overflows into rigidity and everything becomes serious. Relentless comedy or endless tragedy disintegrates the creative self as a living system, so God's image in the deep current is obscured or lost.

The tragic hero's seriousness might arouse pity and fear, but heroic *rigidity* (blind, prideful, compulsive commitment to a cause) can easily destroy the hero as well as those near and even dear. We are drawn toward tragic people because of their sacrifice and leadership, but at the same time something makes us draw back. This "drawing back" is our impulse toward life and the need to return to the deep channel. The narrow focus of the hero on the task and the willingness to sacrifice others to reach the goal rests on rigidity. The goal of the hero may be very important and of great benefit to others, but it is the way the goal is sought that makes it destructive rather than constructive.

Tragic heroes need a healthy dose of comedy to lend them some self-awareness and community to prevent getting hopelessly stuck in the rigidity of narcissism. The decay of Tolkien's Saruman is an example of this privation. Staying in touch with comedy also helps make one more effective and creative to accomplish the heroic task. Tragedy and comedy need each other for creativity to flow.

Comedy can also take over one's life. The comedic experience of life begins lightly with the integration of the main character into society. While a tragedy might end with people dying on stage, a comedy ends with people coming together and even getting married. A tragedy arouses pity and fear while a comedy arouses sympathy and playful teasing.

The danger of comedy is not comedy itself. As with tragedy, the danger is getting stuck. When comedy becomes compulsive, it no longer brings the fresh air of freedom into one's life and creativity to one's outlook. Sympathy for others is diminished and one's authentic sense of humor is strangled. Even the union of marriage and being integrated into one's society gets contemptuously and sarcastically dismissed. Drifting over the bank past comedy into chaos blocks creativity, because it is no longer in touch with the structure and responsibility needed to give it life.

Listening to the laughter and tears of children and adults is like listening to the turbulence of life's flowing river.[31] Henri Bergson conceived of life is a "vital impulse," an élan vital. When it loses its fluidity and becomes mechanical, we are likely to hear warning laughter, and I would add, see tears of frustration. Bergson thought this was because we are no longer "ceaselessly adapting and readapting" and the self "slackens in the attention that is due to life." This results in mechanical movement without life.[32] The resulting laughter or tears awakens us to an awareness of life's flow and the need to move back into the deep channel.

This is why the laughter and tears of children and adults are so important. They are the nonverbal language system that shows us when and how to steer back into the deep channel. These profound signs signal when we need to re-integrate the four dimensions of the creative process and become part of a community of creativity to sustain us. They show where God's kingdom can be found.

---

31. The laughter of wonder, the laughter of delight, and the satisfied smile of soft closure are the signs that creativity is running in the deep channel. Laughter needs no words to communicate its meaning so it can be shared by children and adults. Children often live in the deep channel unconsciously, but adults need to integrate the whole person—psychologically, socially, biologically, and spiritually—to live there.

A "laugh" is not a person, place, or thing. It is a unique kind of communication that involves corporality, time, and place. We know what laughter means with our bodies and our spirits. After we laugh and reflect on our laughter, we can know what it means with our minds. The laughter of wonder and the laughter of delight signal that the creative process is flowing well. This realization comes to us from beyond, from beside, and from within when the inner creativity of the Holy Trinity spills over into our creating and we respond, hurrying toward the presence of the Creator that we came from as part of God's creating. This is what we return to at the end of our days.

32. There are many printings of Bergson's *Laughter*. Wylie Sypher edited my favorite edition, which might be overlooked because of the complexity of its title. It is called *Comedy: An Essay on Comedy by George Meredith and Laughter by Henri Bergson with an Introduction and Appendix "The Meaning of Comedy" by Wylie Sypher* (Baltimore MD: The Johns Hopkins University Press, 1956), 187.

CONCLUSION

We have explored Jesus' invitation to become like a child from five different perspectives. We have lived our way into the child/adult paradox, described the child we are to be like, played with parable children to expand our understanding of human creativity and re-creation, absorbed the promise of union with the Creator, and reflected on how to cope with losing our way in the river of life.

We have discovered that to be mature beyond the norm we need to be able to steer between chaos and rigidity, drawing on both, because that is where our deepest identity is with God and the community of creating. This is what being in the kingdom is like for children and adults and what children can teach adults when we forget what we once knew. The kingdom is always there at all levels of experience from affinity with God to planning what to have for supper.

There is one more step we need to take to finish our journey. We need to respond with art to the whole experience of the book to provide a soft closure. This ending which is also a beginning will extend Jesus' aphorism into a fable, which will be found in the next chapter.

An "art response" merely expresses the soft closure. It is not a summing up that closes the discussion. It continues to participate in what has taken place but at the same time points to the future, as we continue to move forward with the charioteer, who guides the four horses and the chariot, toward a meaningful home.

You might want to dance *your* "art response," or maybe your response will be a deeper rapport with nature. It might be visual and spatial, like a painting or sculpture. Perhaps your soft closure will be interpersonal and social, or draw on your unique sensitivity to the inner, personal world of individuals. You may prefer logic and math or music and rhythm. You might want to create a spiritual practice to embody your response or enact a deeply moral project.

I can't anticipate what you will do as part of the community of creating encouraged by this book. That is up to you. All I can say is that my art response will be found in the next chapter as an invitation for you to complete your own.

CHAPTER 6

A Stable Nativity

RESPONDING TO JESUS' CREATION

The Cathedral stood on a high promontory. Its spire pointed beyond the vanishing point. Inside the stone shape, Hide and Seek was played each week. Sometimes God hid. Sometimes people did. The truth of both hiding and seeking was found when bread and wine were shared—tasting of grace, time, and space.

One day a priest walked through the long, gothic nave, carefully inspecting the sacred precincts. He entered the narthex, the space between the nave and the great door, where sojourners went in and out. Next to the ceremonial door was a smaller, interior one, whose oak was now harder than the iron of its hinges. The priest stood in front of the small door for a moment and then took out a large black key he kept with him. It turned with difficulty in the lock. He then pulled open the heavy door.

Down he went around the circular, stone staircase into the deepest part of the structure below the great tower. At the bottom was a musty, dim room. An elaborate carving sat at its center. The wood was gnarled, yet etched with intricate art. People saw many things in its contours. It had strong legs with clawed feet, but where the seat ought to have been was a rough-hewn box, which made sitting awkward. The back looked like a cross with equal extensions, the two on the sides reached forward like the arms of a person. As the carving crouched there, it seemed to subtly shift in shape and color—but all this had been discussed before. Now the priests hardly noticed it. What they did notice was when something was amiss. Today something was.

The priest looked suspiciously around the room. There! A tiny, almost transparent plant was pushing its tendrils up between the stones beneath the feet of the gnarled wood. He knelt and tried to pull it out by its roots, but it would not budge. He tried to snap it off like a glass straw, but it bent like soft plastic. With a prayer he cut it off cleanly with a sharp knife, to make the space immaculate once more. The priest climbed back up the stairs, strangely sweating and shaking. A few days went by, but the incident kept coming vividly to mind. The priest went back to see for himself, if all were well. It was not.

The plant had grown once more above the level of the floor. He cut it down again, and, on succeeding days, again and again. Soon, all the priests knew it was true. When you trimmed the growth it grew stronger. A special council was called. It was decided that the offense must be buried beneath a new floor, laid over the old one. Stonemasons were summoned and the work was done. The wooden carving was returned to the center of the room.

The following week the inspecting priest unlocked the oak door and descended the stone stairway. He was so shocked by what he saw that he could barely struggle back up the stairs to shout for help. The black robed figures hurried down into the circular room, each carrying a lantern. They saw hundreds of slender, transparent runners glistening among the stones in the flickering light. Small rocks came loose and clattered to the floor. It was worse than anyone could imagine. The growth was escaping!

The priests became frantic. Workmen were called that very night. Stones were carried into the church by torchlight and rolled down into the depths. Soon the whole room was filled with rocks and cement. Then, during the dark days of winter, the doorway was sealed. Iron pins secured the stones. The ancient, gnarled carving was forgotten in a crypt.

By the time the snow slid with a crash from the green copper roof in spring, the victory seemed won. The people of the village had not been told about the struggle, but they had seen it. "What was all that rock for?" they wondered. As the weather warmed, their minds turned to other things—crops and shops, kitchens and cribs.

During the summer the usual midweek Mass was very quiet, since only a few people came to pray. You could almost hear the sunlight sliding through the glass and bursting into colors, until, one day, the faint sound of weeping was heard. No one crying could be found.

A few weeks later, traces of moisture began to shine on the great, east window, high above the main altar. The vast, glass Mary, gazing into the empty tomb, glistened. There was no natural explanation.

The sound of weeping grew stronger as the summer passed. By fall, moisture ran like tears down the front window. A priest put his finger into the water and tasted it, as a joke, to see if it were salty. It was.

Soon, many strangers came to the church. They mixed with the community to hear the weeping and see the tears running down the glass. In their devotion, they missed the small cracks that began to appear in the walls, but when the great beams above them groaned, they were startled and looked up. The vaulted ceiling above them was too high for them to see how dangerously strained the vibrating timbers were.

In late autumn a fine dust settled over everything in the church. No matter how much cleaning was done, more was needed. The dust sifted into the holy bread and wine and into the stiff collars of the priests. Everyone was uncomfortable, but the people did not stop coming until their pious curiosity turned to fear.

By winter the wood shrieked. The building shuddered. No songs were sung, nor services said. Nothing could be heard inside but splintering wood, the creaking roof, and falling stones.

On Christmas morning the clergy tried to celebrate the birth of Christ in the devastation, but when they entered the chaotic church they were stunned. During the night the roof had split open! Bits of slate and copper still banged and clattered against the stone floor and broken pews. Above them was the winter sky.

They tried to absorb and understand what was happening as huge pieces of wood, chunks of rock, and fragments of plaster fell everywhere like an avalanche. Even the bells began to fall—crashing and ringing—inside the great spire. The whole structure was breaking up! The priests ran frantically into the snow, their robes flying behind them.

When they could run no further, they stood, panting and gasping for air in the cold. Their frosty breath circled them as they turned fearfully around to look at the church. As they watched, the great tower let itself down with immense dignity. It did not topple over. It came down inside itself, catching its own rubble as it fell.

A dark cloud of destruction swept over the priests. They shivered from panic and ached with cold. Tears came to their eyes. The earth trembled beneath them. Their ears throbbed with blood as they stood lost in the swirling dust that obscured the sacred place they had known so well. A breeze came up. The cloud began to thin. What they saw sent them to their knees, making the sign of the cross.

Most saw a broken shell, shattered beyond repair. Many shook their heads and muttered. A few went away silent, angry, and sad. But some said they saw an almost transparent shape, something like a tree, rising as tall as the old tower.

It began to snow. The silent drifts smoothed over the ruin, which lay alone all winter. No one had the courage to think about it. There was too much brokenness to risk caring.

In the spring people began to return to the rubble of the church. Wide-eyed children heard tiny chimes above them as they played in the ruins, occasionally glimpsing a canopy of leaves only seen in flashes of sunlight. They sensed a faint laughter, more felt than heard, as they ran and skipped among the stones. More children came. They played with chunks of colored glass, slate, copper, stone, wood, brass, and the scattered pages of torn books. They held these fragments up to the light for fun and put them together in new ways. The tree gradually gained reality, and the birds of the air came to nest there. The desolation became a playground. Adults watched with unexplained happiness.

One day a child pressed a piece of broken glass into the tree most adults could not see. It stuck tight. What fun! Something had begun. The embedded fragments stayed. When people tried to pry them out, they could not. The children kept pressing tiny piece after tiny piece timelessly into the presence of the tree, until its shape was there for everyone to see.

Some adults struggled to smother the children's wonder. "This cannot happen," they said. "Physics and politics do not allow such things." The children's smiles defied such thoughts, and the shape ascended despite all natural and social law.

Slowly, over the years, the bits and pieces of the shattered church grew together into a mixture of old and new, until it was whole again. It was strong and tall with open doors. People went inside and rested in the shade. The wind, the ringing leaves, and the songs of birds were transposed into breathing organ pipes, vibrating bells, and voices. It was too good and too beautiful to be true. But there it was! It was doing, once again, what churches do best—*exuberance*.

Decades of decades went by and the new church became old again. The stable movement of its creativity, like a river's flow, slowly became fixed like crystal. The lovely, living, liturgical year, expressing creativity *itself*, became an artificial, wind-up toy, ornamenting the passing days. Without anyone meaning to, the openness of the church began to close and settled into the rigidity of the stones.

A few days before Christmas, a priest took a key from her ring and unlocked a small but ponderous door. She climbed down around the winding stairs with great care into the stone depths beneath the church's tower. The priest moved with difficulty, holding on to the railing, because she was great with child, nearly to term. She had hoped to celebrate the Feast of the Incarnation with joy in the Cathedral, but the joy of her baby might arrive instead.

When she stepped onto the circular, stone floor, she looked around. Everything seemed in order, but she was very weary and unsteady. Without thinking she leaned on the old, chair-shaped thing in the middle of the room. She would have sat down if there had been a proper seat, but something like an ancient feed box already sat there between the arms, so it was impossible. After she rested she noticed that something was growing up between the stones under the gnarled carving. It was almost transparent. She straightened up, suddenly alert, and watched, happily, as it grew. It stopped, then slowly with-drew, and disappeared. That was strange.

She leaned again on the carving. That was when she noticed a faint humming in the stones around her. It made her smile. The stones seemed to relax. In her reverie she heard the sound of someone bounding down the stairs. It was the new, young curate. He had grown up nearby. His family had lived close to the Cathedral for many, many generations.

"There you are! I was worried. Let me help you back up the stairs. Don't you think you should go home? The baby is coming soon."

"I am trying to wait until after Christmas. I want to help with the celebration."

"You *are* helping! Let's climb back up the stairs together. Things are fine here."

And they still are.

BIBLIOGRAPHY

Agamben, Giorgio. *Infancy and History: On the Destruction of Experience*. London: Verso, 2007.

———. *The Church and the Kingdom*. Calcutta: Seagull Books, 2012.

Alighieri, Dante. *Purgatorio*. Translated by Charles S. Singleton. Princeton, NJ: Princeton University Press, 1973.

Andreasen, Nancy C. *Creating Brain: The Neuroscience of Genius*. New York: Dana Press, 2005.

———. "Secrets of the Creative Brain." *The Atlantic*, August 2014.

Arendt, Hannah. *Eichmann in Jerusalem: A Report on the Banality of Evil*. New York: Viking Press, 1963.

Aries, Philippe. *A History of Private Life*. Edited by Philippe Aries and Georges Duby. 5 vols. Cambridge, MA: Harvard University Press, 1992.

———. *L'Enfant et La Vie Familiale Sous l'Ancien Regime* (*Centuries of Childhood*), Paris: Librairie Plon, 1960.

———. *Western Attitudes Toward Death*. Baltimore: The Johns Hopkins University Press, 1974.

Arieti, Silvano. *Creativity: The Magical Synthesis*. New York: Basic Books, 1976.

Aristotle. *Organon*, n.d.

Augustine. *Confessions*. Translated by Henry Chadwick. Oxford, UK: Oxford University Press, World's Classics edition, 1992.

———. *Reconsiderations*, n.d.

Bacon, Francis. *Novum Organum Scientiarum* (*The New Tool for Science*). Vol. 1, 1620.

Balthasar, Hans Urs von. *Our Task*. San Francisco: Ignatius Press, 1984.

———. *The Glory of the Lord: A Theological Aesthetics, V: The Realm of Metaphysics in the Modern Age*. San Francisco: Ignatius Press, 1991.

———. *Unless You Become Like This Child*. Cambridge, MA: Harvard University Press, 2004.

———. *Unless You Become Like This Child*. unpublished, n.d.

Barth, Karl. *Protestant Theology in the Nineteenth Century: Its Background and History*. King of Prussia, PA: Judson Press, 1973.

Berryman, Jerome. *Children and the Theologians*. New York: Morehouse Publishing, 2009.

———. "Laughter, Power, and Motivation in Religious Education." *Religious Education* 93, no. 3 (1998): 358–378.

———. *Teaching Godly Play: How to Mentor the Spiritual Development of Children*. Denver, CO: Morehouse Education Resources, 2009.

———. *The Complete Guide to Godly Play*. Vol. 3. 8 vols. Denver, CO: Morehouse Education Resources, 2002.

———. "The Nonverbal Nature of Spirituality and Religious Language in Spiritual Education." Edited by J. Erricker, C. Ota, and C. Erricker. Brighton, UK: Sussex Academic Press, 2001.

———. *The Search for a Theology of Childhood: Essays by Jerome W. Berryman from 1978–2009*. Edited by Brendan Hyde. Ballarat, VIC, Australia: Mondotti Press (an Imprint of Connor Court Publishing), 2013.

———. *The Spiritual Guidance of Children: Montessori, Godly Play, and the Future*. New York: Morehouse Publishing, 2013.

———. "The Transforming Moment and Godly Play." In *The Logic of the Spirit in Human Thought and Experience*, edited by Dana R. Wright and Keith J. White. Eugene, OR: Pickwick Publications, Wipf and Stock Publishers, 2014.

Blake, William. "'Auguries of Innocence' from 'The Pickering Manuscript,'" 1863.

Bloom, Paul. *Just Babies: The Origins of Good and Evil*. New York: Crown Publishers, 2013.

Book of Kells, 9th century.

Breech, James. *The Silence of Jesus: The Authentic Voice of the Historical Man*. Minneapolis, MN: Fortress Press, 1983.

Brenner, William H. "Chesterton, Wittgenstein and the Foundations of Ethics." *Philosophical Investigations* 14, no. 4 (October 1991).

Brown, Peter. *Augustine of Hippo*. Berkeley, CA: University of California Press, 1967.

Brown, Stuart. *Play: How It Shapes the Brain, Opens the Imagination, and Invigorates the Soul*. New York: Penguin, 2009.

Bunyan, John. *The Pilgrim's Progress*, n.d.

Buruma, Ian. *Year Zero: A History of 1945*. New York: Penguin Press, 2013.

Capobianco, Richard. *Heidegger's Way of Being*. Toronto: University of Toronto Press, 2014.

Castiglione, Baldasar. *Book of the Courtier*, 1528.

Center for History and New Media. "Zotero Quick Start Guide," n.d. *http://zotero.org/support/quick_start_guide*

Chadwick, Henry. *Saint Augustine: Confessions.* Oxford, UK: Oxford Paperbacks, 2009.

Chesterton, G. K. "The Ethics of Elfland." In *Orthodoxy*, 1908.

Clark, Arthur C. *2001: A Space Odyssey*, n.d.

Coe, Richard N. *When the Grass Was Taller: Autobiography and the Experience of Childhood.* New Haven, CT: Yale University Press, 1984.

Cooper, Mick. *Existential Therapies.* London: Sage Publications, 2003.

Countryman, L. William. *The Poetic Imagination.* London: Longman and Todd Ltd., 1999.

Crossan, John Dominic. *Cliffs of Fall: Paradox and Polyvalence in the Parables of Jesus.* New York: The Seabury Press, 1980.

———. *Dark Interval.* Sonoma, CA: Polebridge Press, 1994.

———. *Finding Is the First Act.* Eugene, OR: Wipf and Stock, 2008.

———. *In Fragments: The Aphorisms of Jesus.* San Francisco: Harper and Row, 1983.

———. *In Parables: The Challenge of the Historical Jesus.* Sonoma, CA: Polebridge Press, 1992.

———. *Jesus: A Revolutionary Biography.* New York: HarperSanFrancisco, 1994.

———. *The Historical Jesus.* New York: HarperCollins, 1993.

Csikszentmihalyi, Mihaly. *The Evolving Self: A Psychology for the Third Millennium.* New York: Harper Perennial, 1993.

Cunningham, Hugh. *Children and Childhood in Western Society Since 1500.* London: Longman, 1995.

———. *The Invention of Childhood.* London: BBC Books, 2006.

de Mause, Lloyd. *The History of Childhood.* New York: Psychohistory Press, 1974.

Dillenberger, John. *God Hidden and Revealed.* Philadelphia: Muhlenberg Press, 1953.

Donoghue, Denis. *Metaphor.* Cambridge, MA: Harvard University Press, 2014.

Dostoyevsky, Fyodor. *The Brothers Karamazov*, 1880.

Dowell, Graham. *Enjoying the World: The Rediscovery of Thomas Traherne.* Harrisburg, PA: Morehouse Publishing, 1990.

Eco, Umberto. *Kant and the Platypus: Essays on Language and Cognition.* New York: Harcourt, A Harvest Book, 2000.

Elias, Eileen. *On Sundays We Wore White: Childhood Reminiscences.* Redhill, Surrey: Love & Malcomson, 1978.

Erricker, Jane, and Cathy Ota. *Spiritual Education: Cultural, Religious and Social Differences; New Perspectives in the 21st Century.* Brighton, UK: Sussex Academic Press, 2001.

Feuerbach, Ludwig. *The Essence of Christianity (Das Wesen Des Christentums)*. Translated by George Elliot. New York: Harper & Brothers Publishers, 1841.

Frost, Robert. "Mending Wall" (poem), n.d.

Frye, Northrop. *Anatomy of Criticism*. Princeton, NJ: Princeton University Press, 1957.

Gardner, Howard. *Creating Minds: An Anatomy of Creativity Seen Through the Lives of Freud, Einstein, Picasso, Stravinsky, Eliot, Graham, and Gandhi*. New York: Basic Books, 1993.

Garvey, Catherine. *Play: The Developing Child*. Second edition. Cambridge, MA: Harvard University Press, 1990.

Gergan, Kenneth J. *The Saturated Self*. New York: Basic Books, 1991.

Gill, Jean. *Unless You Become Like a Little Child*. New York: Paulist Press, 1985.

Goleman, Daniel. *Emotional Intelligence*. New York: Bantam, 2005.

Gopnik, Alison. *The Philosophical Baby*. New York: Picador, 2009.

Harding, Thomas. *Hanns and Rudolf: The True Story of the German Jew Who Tracked Down and Caught the Kommandant of Auschwitz*. New York: Simon and Schuster, 2013.

Heidegger, Martin. *What Is Called Thinking?*, 1951.

Heller, Joseph. *Catch-22*, n.d.

Hoff, Johannes. *The Analogical Turn: Rethinking Modernity with Nicholas of Cusa*. Grand Rapids, MI: Wm. B. Eerdmans Publishing Co., 2013.

Jacob. *Mystical Theology*, 5th century.

Jeremias, Joachim. *The Parables of Jesus*. Second edition. New York: Charles Scribner's Sons, 1972.

Kahneman, Daniel. *Thinking, Fast and Slow*. New York: Farrar, Straus and Giroux, 2011.

Kappus, Franz Xaver. *Letters to a Young Poet*, 1929.

Kaufman, Gordon. *In Face of Mystery*. Kaufman, 1993.

———. "On Thinking of God as Serendipitous Creativity." *Journal of the American Academy of Religion*, 2001.

Kelber, Werner. *The Oral and the Written Gospel: The Hermeneutics of Speaking and Writing in the Synoptic Tradition, Mark, Paul, and Q*. Philadelphia: Fortress Press, 1983.

Kessel, Frank L., and Alexander W. Siegel, eds. *The Child and Other Cultural Inventions*. New York: Praeger Publishers, 1983.

Kessen, William. "Presidential Address to the American Psychological Association's Division of Developmental Psychological," 1978.

———. "The American Child and Other Cultural Inventions." *American Psychologist* 34 (1979): 815–820.

Kierkegaard, Søren. *The Concept of Anxiety: A Simple Psychologically Orienting Deliberation on the Dogmatic Issue of Hereditary Sin*. Princeton, NJ: Princeton University Press, 1980.

King, Thomas M., SJ. *Teilhard's Mass: Approaches to "The Mass on the World."* New York/Mahwah, NJ: Paulist Press, 2005.

Kissinger, Warren S. *The Parables of Jesus: A History of Interpretation and Bibliography*. Metuchen, NJ: The Scarecrow Press, 1979.

Lesmoir-Gordon, Nigel, Will Rood, and Ralph Edney. *Fractals: A Graphic Guide*. London: Icon Books, 2009.

Lewis, C. S. *The Four Loves*, n.d.

Lewis, Thomas, Fari Amini, and Richard Lannon. *A General Theory of Love*. New York: Random House, 2000.

Louv, Richard. *Childhood's Future*. New York: Doubleday, 1991.

———. *Last Child in the Woods: Saving Our Children from Nature Deficit Disorder*. Chapel Hill, NC: Algonquin Books of Chapel Hill, 2008.

Lubac, Henri de. *Paradoxes of Faith*. San Francisco: Ignatius Press, 1987.

Lutz, Tom. *Crying: The Natural and Cultural History of Tears*. New York: W.W. Norton and Co., 1999.

Lyubomirsky, Sonja. *The How of Happiness*. New York: Penguin Press HC, 2007.

MacCulloch, Diarmaid. *Silence: A Christian History*. New York: Penguin Books, 2013.

MacDonald, Margaret Y. *The Power of Children: The Construction of Christian Families in the Greco-Roman World*. Waco, TX: Baylor University Press, 2014.

Macquarrie, John. *Principles of Christian Theology*. Second edition. New York: Scribner & Sons, 1977.

Mandelbrot, Benoit. *Fractals: Form, Chance, and Dimension*. San Francisco: W. H. Freeman and Company, 1977.

———. *The Fractalist: Memoir of a Scientific Maverick*. New York: Vintage Books, 2013.

Mathewes, Charles T. *Evil and the Augustinian Tradition*. Cambridge : Cambridge University Press, 2001.

Mavomatis, Andreas. *Hypnagogia: The Unique State Between Wakefulness and Sleep*. Third edition. Thyrsos Press, 2010.

Merkur, Dan. *Mystical Moments and Unitive Thinking*. Albany, NY: State University of New York Press, 1999.

Miller, David L. *Christs: Meditations on Archetypal Images in Christian Theology*. New York: The Seabury Press, 1981.

Mintz, Stephen. *Huck's Raft: A History of American Childhood*. Cambridge, MA: Harvard University Press, n.d.

Mithen, Steven. *The Prehistory of the Mind: The Cognitive Origins of Art, Religion, and Science.* London: Phoenix Paperback, 1998.

Mooney, Timothy J. *Becoming Like a Child: Restoring the Awe, Wonder, Joy & Resiliency of the Human Spirit.* Woodstock, VT: Christian Journeys from Skylight Paths Publishing, 2014.

Neiman, Susan. *Evil in Modern Thought: An Alternative Story of Philosophy.* Princeton, NJ: Princeton University Press, 2002.

Niebuhr, Reinhold. *Moral Man and Immoral Society*, 1932.

O'Donnell, James J. *Augustine: A New Biography.* New York: Harper Perennial, 2006.

Panksepp, Jaak, and Lucy Biven. *The Archeology of the Mind: Neuro-evolutionary Origins of Human Emotions.* New York: W.W. Norton and Co., 2012.

Perrin, Norman. *Jesus and the Kingdom*, n.d.

———. *Jesus and the Language of the Kingdom: Symbol and Metaphor in New Testament Interpretation.* Philadelphia: Fortress Press, 1976.

Pfenninger, Karl, and Valerie Shubik, eds. *The Origins of Creativity.* Oxford, UK: Oxford University Press, 2001.

Plato. *Plato The Symposium.* Translated by W. Hamilton. Baltimore: Penguin Books, 1951.

Pollack, Linda. *Forgotten Children: Parent-Child Relations from 1500–1900.* Cambridge: Cambridge University Press, 1983.

Postman, Neil. *Disappearance of Childhood.* New York: Vintage Books, 1994.

———. *The Disappearance of Childhood.* New York: Vintage Books, 1982.

Pridmore, John. *Playing with Icons: The Spirituality of a Recalled Childhood.* Unpublished, private mss., 2015.

Ramsey, Ian T. *Religious Language: An Empirical Placing of Theological Phrases.* London: SCM Press, 1957.

Richard of St. Victor. *The Twelve Patriarchs; The Mystical Ark; Book Three of the Trinity.* Translated by Grover A. Zinn. New York: Paulist Press, 1979.

Sawyer, Keith R. *Explaining Creativity: The Science of Human Innovation.* Second edition. Oxford, UK: Oxford University Press, 2012.

Scheffler, Johann. *The Cherubinic Wanderer*, 1657.

Schindler, David L. *Hans Urs von Balthasar: His Life and Work,.* San Francisco: Communio, 1991.

Schweitzer, Albert. *The Quest of the Historical Jesus.* New York: The Macmillan Company, 1964.

Scott, Bernard Brandon. *Hear Then the Parable: A Commentary on the Parables of Jesus.* Minneapolis, MN: Fortress Press, 1989.

Scott, Joanna Vecchiarelli, and Judith Chelius Stark, eds. *Hannah Arendt: Love and Saint Augustine*. Chicago: University of Chicago Press, 1996.

Shakespeare, William. *Romeo and Juliet*, n.d.

Sheehan, Thomas. "Heidegger and Christianity." In *The Cambridge Dictionary of Christianity*, edited by Daniel Patte. Cambridge: Cambridge University Press, 2010.

Shippey, Tom. *J. R. R. Tolkien: Author of the Century*. New York: Houghton Mifflin, 2002.

Siegel, Daniel J. *Pocket Guide to Interpersonal Neurobiology*. New York: W.W. Norton and Co., 2012.

Sommerville, John. *The Rise and Fall of Childhood*. Beverly Hills, CA: Sage Publications, 1982.

Stevens, Wallace. *The Necessary Angel: Essays on Reality and the Imagination*. New York: Knopf and Random House, Vintage Books, 1951.

Stossel, Scott. *My Age of Anxiety: Fear, Hope, Dread, and the Search for Peace of Mind*. New York: Alfred A. Knopf, 2014.

St. Thomas. *Summa Theologiae*, n.d.

Sunstein, Cass R. "Who Knows If You're Happy?" *The New York Review*, December 4, 2014.

Sutton-Smith, Brian. *The Ambiguity of Play*. Cambridge, MA: Harvard University Press, 1997.

Swift, Jonathan. *Gulliver's Travels*, n.d.

Sypher, Wylie. *Comedy: An Essay on Comedy, George Meredith and Laughter, Henri Bergson: Introduction and Appendix "The Meaning of Comedy" by Wylie Sypher*. Baltimore: The Johns Hopkins University Press, 1956.

Tawney, R. H. *Religion and the Rise of Capitalism*, n.d.

Teilhard de Chardin, Pierre. "The Mass on the World," n.d.

Terrien, Samuel. *The Elusive Presence: Toward a New Biblical Theology*. Eugene, OR: Wipf and Stock, 2000.

Thaler, Richard H., and Cass R. Sunstein. *Nudge*. New Haven, CT: Yale University Press, 2008.

Thomas, Aquinas. "Eucharistic Hymn," thirteenth century.

Thomas, R. S. *Poems of R. S. Thomas*. Fayetteville, AR: The University of Arkansas Press, 1985.

Thompson, Francis. *The Hound of Heaven in the Norton Anthology of English Literature*. Edited by M. H. Abrams. First edition. Vol. 2. New York: W.W. Norton and Co., 1962.

————. "The Kingdom of God," n.d.

Tolkien, J. R. R. *The Lord of the Rings*. London: HarperCollins, 2004.

Traherne, Thomas. *Christian Ethicks*, n.d.

Turner, Denys. *The Darkness of God: Negativity in Christian Mysticism*. Cambridge: Cambridge University Press, 1995.

———. *Thomas Aquinas: A Portrait*. New Haven, CT: Yale University Press, 2013.

Vaillant, George. *Adaptation to Life*. Cambridge, MA: Harvard University Press, 1977.

———. *Triumphs of Experience: The Men of the Harvard Grant Study*. Cambridge, MA: The Belknap Press of Harvard University Press, 2012.

Vaughn, Henry. *The World*, n.d.

Vermes, Geza. *Jesus the Jew: A Historian's Reading of the Gospels*. Philadelphia: Fortress Press, 1973.

Weber, Hans-Ruedi. *Jesus and the Children: Biblical Resources for Study and Preaching*. Geneva: World Council of Churches, 1979.

Weiss, Johannes. "Jesus' Proclamation of the Kingdom of God," 1892.

Weitzenhoffer, Andre Muller. *The Practice of Hypnotism*. Second edition. New York: John Wiley & Sons, 2000.

Wells, Samuel. "In an Urban Estate." In *Faithfulness and Fortitude: In Conversation with the Theological Ethics of Stanley Hauerwas*, edited by Mark Thiessen Nation and Samuel Wells. Edinburgh: T and T Clark, 2000.

Whitehead, Alfred North. *Process and Reality*, 1927.

Wiesel, Elie. *One Generation After*. New York: Schocken Books, 1965.

Wiman, Christian. *My Bright Abyss: Meditation of a Modern Believer*. New York: Farrar, Straus and Giroux, 2013.

Winnicott, D. W. *Playing and Reality*. London: Tavistock Publications, 1985.

Woolf, Virginia. *Moments of Being: A Collection of Autobiographical Writing*. Edited by Jeanne Schulkind. Second edition. San Diego, CA: Harcourt, A Harvest Book, 1985.

Wordsworth, William. "My Heart Leaps Up" ("The Rainbow"), 1802.

Yagoda, Ben. *Memoir: A History*. New York: Riverhead Books, 2009.

Yalom, Irving. *Existential Psychotherapy*. New York: Basic Books, 1980.

INDEX